Is Racism a Serious Problem?

Jeff Plunkett, *Book Editor*

Bruce Glassman, *Vice President*
Bonnie Szumski, *Publisher*
Helen Cothran, *Managing Editor*

OPPOSING
VIEWPOINTS®
SERIES

GREENHAVEN PRESS
An imprint of Thomson Gale, a part of The Thomson Corporation

THOMSON

™

GALE

Detroit • New York • San Francisco • San Diego • New Haven, Conn.
Waterville, Maine • London • Munich

For more information, contact
Greenhaven Press
27500 Drake Rd.
Farmington Hills, MI 48331-3535
Or you can visit our Internet site at http://www.gale.com

LIBRARY OF CONGRESS CATALOGING-IN-PUBLICATION DATA

Is racism a serious problem? / Jeff Plunkett, book editor.
   p. cm. — (At issue)
Includes bibliographical references and index.
ISBN 0-7377-2400-5 (lib. : alk. paper) — ISBN 0-7377-2401-3 (pbk. : alk. paper)
   1. Racism—United States. 2. United States—Race relations. I. Plunkett, Jeff.
II. At issue (San Diego, Calif.)
E184.A1I174 2005
305.8'00973—dc22
                                                  2004053932

Printed in the United States of America

Contents

Introduction

The United States does not have a proud history of race relations. At the start of the Civil War, in 1861, nearly 4 million African Americans were legally enslaved in America. Though the Thirteenth Amendment officially abolished slavery in 1865, widespread discrimination persisted. In 1892, Homer Plessy, a shoemaker from Louisiana who was one-eighth black, was thrown in jail for sitting in a "white" railway car. His subsequent appeal to the Supreme Court, in *Plessy v. Ferguson*, resulted in the landmark decision that racial segregation was legal as long as states provided "separate but equal" facilities, a ruling that set the stage for the legalized racism of the Jim Crow South for the next sixty years. During World War I and World War II, African Americans fought to preserve the ideals of democracy around the world but returned home to a country that did not treat its own citizens with equal respect. Racism often took murderous form: Between 1882 and 1951, almost thirty-five hundred blacks were lynched in the United States.

In 1954, though, things began to change. In that year, the U.S. Supreme Court struck down the "separate but equal" doctrine of the *Plessy* case and required—in *Brown v. Board of Education*—the desegregation of schools. This decision is often considered the beginning of the civil rights movement. Other historic events would soon erode barriers to integration—the Montgomery, Alabama, bus boycotts of 1955; student sit-ins at "white only" lunch counters throughout the South; Martin Luther King Jr.'s 1963 "I have a dream" speech in Washington, D.C.; and, eventually, the Civil Rights Act of 1964 and the Voting Rights Act of 1965. African Americans still faced widespread inequalities in education, employment, housing, and income, but public awareness of the ill effects of racism was heightened by the new medium of television, which broadcast the atrocities of southern racism into the nation's living rooms, and the court system was at last protecting the civil rights of black America.

These events are the basic curriculum of American history classes. Typically, students learn about America's racist past— slavery, forced segregation, lynching—and then are introduced to a group of courageous black Americans (such as King, and Rosa Parks, who refused to give up her bus seat) who led a non-violent movement for equality. It is a hopeful and somewhat simplistic story: Americans made mistakes and then learned from those mistakes and American society today is enlightened and stronger. But the truth is far more complicated. As Americans celebrate the fiftieth anniversary of the *Brown v. Board of Education* decision, the answer to the question "Is racism a serious problem?" is not clear.

Evidence for and against continuing racism

Some argue that the absence of overt acts of bigotry, like the lynchings from the early twentieth century, is proof of drastic change. They point to statistics such as the rise in education levels (the U.S. Census Bureau reports that 80 percent of blacks aged twenty-five and older were high school graduates in 2002, compared with just 30 percent in 1968) and the achievements of blacks such as respected political figures Condoleezza Rice, President George W. Bush's national security adviser, and Secretary of State Colin Powell, as proof that the country is on the right track.

Others claim that racism continues to haunt the country in more subtle ways that are no less serious. Currently, black men make up 41 percent of the inmates in federal, state, and local prisons but account for only 4 percent of all students in American institutions of higher education. In 2002, an average black household had a net worth of $19,000 compared with $121,000 for whites. Many people claim that such disparities would not exist in a truly equal society. Paul Streets, for example, explains in his Znet.org article *"Brown v. Board 50 Years Out"* how institutionalized racism works in twenty-first-century America. According to Streets, there are rich white school districts in suburban Chicago that spend as much as $18,000 per year per student. Across town, in poor black neighborhoods, districts spend less than $7,000:

> This reflects a privilege-preserving school-funding system that bases per-student expenditures largely on the local property tax base—a wonderful U.S. formula that is technically "color-blind" but is in fact heavily racialized, thanks to persistent black residential segregation (and discrimination) and per-

sistent huge racial wealth disparities that have deepened considerably since 2001.

Ku Klux Klan marches down Main Street and the "black" and "white" water fountains are a thing of the past, but critics charge institutional racism is thriving in the form of educational inequalities, racial profiling in law enforcement, environmental racism, and an unfair correctional system. In recent years an influx of immigrants, legal and illegal, from Mexico and Latin America has forced towns across America to deal with new integration challenges, and new dynamics of racism. The growth of the Internet is another new factor in modern American race relations. The Web has given racists worldwide a new platform in which to voice hate messages and recruit new believers, yet also offers individuals and groups that aim to fight racism a new tool in communicating civil rights abuses and sharing strategies for shaping a more tolerant society.

The Greenhaven *At Issue: Is Racism a Serious Problem?* considers this debate, examining the scope of racism in modern America and the range of suggested solutions.

1

Racism Is a Serious Problem in the United States

Joe R. Feagin

Joe R. Feagin is Ella McFadden Professor of Liberal Arts in the Department of Sociology at Texas A&M University. An expert in racial, ethnic, and gender relations, Feagin is the coauthor of Ghetto Revolts *(1973), nominated for a Pulitzer Prize, and author of* Living with Racism *and* White Racism: The Basics, *both winners of the Gustavus Myers Center's Outstanding Human Rights Book Award.*

Racism is so deeply embedded in American society that many whites do not recognize it as the serious problem that it is. The foundation for today's racist America lies in the colonial era, when the white majority viewed African Americans as mentally and socially inferior. Whiteness came to be associated with beauty, status, and goodness, and blackness became wholly undesirable, racist attitudes that continue to manifest themselves in hate crimes and discrimination in education, jobs, and housing. A white-to-black, good-to-bad color continuum evolved that influences the way whites react to, oppress, or accept all other people of color. This so-called intermediate racism against Asians and Latinos is no less corrosive than institutionalized white-on-black racism, and ultimately fosters hostility between groups of people of color.

From the beginning a key aspect of the foundation of the United States, and of the colonies earlier, has been a system

Joe R. Feagin, *Systemic Racism: Roots, Current Realities, and Future Reparations.* New York: Routledge, 2000. Copyright © 2000 by Routledge. All rights reserved. Reproduced by permission of Routledge/Taylor & Francis Books, Ltd.

of racism centered substantially in white-on-black oppression. This long-standing structure of racism has been extended and tailored for each new non-European group brought into the sphere of white domination. Thus, U.S. society is not a multiplicity of disconnected racisms directed at peoples of color. Instead, this U.S. society has a central white-supremacist core initially developed in the minds, ideologies, practices, and institutions of those calling themselves "whites" for destroying the indigenous societies and for exploiting African American labor. This structure of racialized domination was later extended and adapted by the descendants of the founders for the oppression of other non-European groups such as Asian and Latino Americans. The critics are justified in criticizing the social sciences, media, and government agencies for not researching or discussing more centrally the racially oppressed situations of Asian and Latino Americans. These and other non-European groups are becoming ever more important to the racial-ethnic mix of the United States, and they do suffer greatly from the white-racist system. However, one must also accent a critical point too often missed by critics of the so-called binary [black-white] paradigm: That white elites and the white public have long evaluated, reacted to, and dominated later non-European entrants coming into the nation from within a previously established and highly imbedded system of antiblack racism. . . .

The foundation: white-on-black oppression

The whites who crafted the foundation of systemic racism were most concerned with the "black race within our bosom," to use James Madison's phrase. Thus, African Americans were the only group brought in large numbers to North America in chains. They were the only group explicitly singled out several times in the U.S. Constitution for coercive control and violent subordination. They were the only group incorporated into the economic and social center of the new society as chattel property from the first century of colonial development. They were placed in a position at the economic center because their labor was used to create the prosperity of the new white-dominated nation. They were the only group viewed by the legal system as having no rights whatsoever, as the 1857 Dred Scott decision [the Supreme Court ruled in part that Negroes had "no rights which any man was bound to respect"] made clear.

White-on-black oppression extended well beyond the economy. It destroyed cultures, families, and heritages. Thus, during slavery and later segregation many black women were sexually assaulted by white men. The children that resulted from these sexual attacks—and most of their descendants—were classified as black under the racist rule of descent. African Americans are the largest racial or ethnic group in North American history to involuntarily lose substantial control over their own procreation—the largest group whose physical makeup was significantly determined over time by the coercive control and sexual assaults of white men: No group has lost so much of its home country ties and cultural heritage. In a pioneering analysis Michael Omi and Howard Winant have argued that the U.S. social system has seen multiple and overlapping "racial formations" that have evolved historically. While this is an important insight, these multiple racial formations are not all of equal significance in the past or present history of U.S. society. The system of antiblack racism is older, deeper, and more central, while other racist arrangements are generally webbed to it or have been shaped by it.

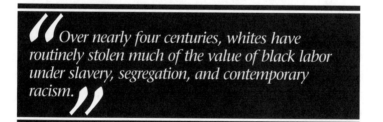

Over nearly four centuries, whites have routinely stolen much of the value of black labor under slavery, segregation, and contemporary racism.

The time of entry, size, distribution, and economic importance of non-European groups have made a difference in the character of their racist incorporation by whites into the society. Note the extent, scale, and location of the oppression of Africans and African Americans over several centuries. Because of their early centrality to the American economic system, African Americans have been more at the core of the white-dominated society than smaller or more regionalized groups. Today, as in the past, sizeable numbers of African Americans are found in more areas of the nation than any other non-European group. Later non-European immigrants, including most Asians and Latinos, have been integrated later and selectively into the U.S. economy and polity—and in fewer places geographically.

Viewed historically, black Americans have been oppressed

much longer by whites than any other group except Native Americans. Over nearly four centuries, whites have routinely stolen much of the value of black labor under slavery, segregation, and contemporary racism. Moreover, the extremely large number of black Americans who were, and are, oppressed underscores the central significance of white-on-black oppression. Between 1619 and 1865 approximately six to seven million black Americans lived under conditions of slavery in North America. Moreover, between 1619 and the year 2000 a total of perhaps sixty to seventy million blacks have lived in North America—and thus have had their labor taken and their lives burdened and truncated by slavery, segregation, and contemporary racism. This rough estimate is larger than for any other group that has suffered racial discrimination at the hands of white Americans.

> *Antiblack racism . . . can be seen . . . in white dominance of the economic, legal, educational, and political arrangements that imbed white interests.*

Another sign of the centrality of white-on-black oppression is the high level of white effort and energy put into maintaining antiblack racism. From the first decades of European colonialism, black Americans have been at the core of the racist system because they are the group whose subjugation has been given the greatest attention by whites. Whites have devoted enormous amounts of energy to oppressing African Americans—initially for labor reasons and later for a range of economic, social, and ideological reasons. Indeed, in the Civil War many thousands of southern whites gave their lives, at least in part, to maintain the enslavement of African Americans. In contrast, whites on the whole have put much less time and physical and mental energy into exploiting and oppressing groups such as Asian and Latino Americans, if only because the latter have been in the United States in large numbers for much shorter periods of time.

Antiblack racism has been reproduced now for several centuries. This reality can be seen not only in the social, economic, and cultural resources passed along generations of white families but also in white dominance of the economic, legal, educational, and political arrangements that imbed white interests. Moreover, once the system of racism was established, substantial individual and collective resistance by black Americans forced whites to put even more effort into maintaining and periodically reframing white-on-black oppression. As some scholars [Jorge Klor de Alva, Earl Shorris, and Cornel West in "Our Next Race Question: The Uneasiness Between Blacks and Latinos"] see it, "One of the reasons why black people are so integral a part of American civilization is because black people have raised a lot of hell.". . .

Rationalizing white-on-black oppression

A thorough racist ideology with its associated prejudices and stereotypes targeting black Americans was created at an early stage in North American history and then was elaborated on in subsequent centuries. By the last decades of the eighteenth century and the early decades of the nineteenth century most whites—from southern slaveholders to northern liberals—agreed on a white-supremacist ideology with two key features: (1) white Europeans have a God-given right to exploit the labor of Africans and African Americans; and (2) the savage and un-Christian "black race" is far inferior to the civilized and Christian "white race." This ideology was not just tacked onto the nation's new institutions; it was an intimate part of the nation's foundation. Since the late eighteenth century whites have developed and extensively utilized this ideology, including those in corner taverns and members of the U.S. Supreme Court. For the first two-and-a-half centuries, numerous laws, including state and federal court decisions, used this ideology in insuring the subordination of black Americans. Moreover, from George Washington in the 1790s to Richard Nixon in the 1970s most U.S. presidents openly expressed antiblack views or took significant antiblack actions based on covertly held stereotyped views. . . .

Even with this focus on African Americans, whites regularly extend ideology of white superiority to other Americans of color, including Native Americans, Latinos, and Asian Americans. . . . The hostile actions generated by this ideology periodically move well beyond verbal attacks—to the stark reality that can be seen in the large number of hate crimes targeting Americans in all these groups over recent decades. . . .

The antiblack orientation is much more than cognitive. . . . Strong emotions, such as fear and loathing, and visual images often undergird the antiblack attitudes of many whites. The racist emotions of these whites seem much weaker in regard to other Americans of color. For example, whites seem to be much less likely to go into defensive maneuvers when an Asian or Latino man is nearby than when a black man is nearby. Whites are also less emotional about interracial marriage when it does not involve whites and blacks.

The racial continuum

The developed and imbedded system of oppression originally created for African Americans has influenced the way whites have reacted to, oppressed, or accepted other people of color. Since the 1850s, one by one, most other non-European groups have been recruited by whites as cheap labor. Yet other immigrants have come as political refugees. Most have originated in societies linked to overseas military operations or imperialism on the part of the United States. Examples of this are China, Japan, and the Philippines in the nineteenth century and Korea, Taiwan, Vietnam, and Cuba in the twentieth. These non-European immigrants and their descendants have frequently been judged and evaluated by whites from within the framework of the white-on-black oppression and ideology already set in place.

> *The treatment of Americans of color has varied according to their time of entry, size, culture, physical characteristics, and wealth.*

Each new immigrant group is usually placed, principally by the dominant whites, somewhere on a *white-to-black status continuum*, the commonplace measuring stick of social acceptability. This socioracial continuum has long been imbedded in white minds, writings, and practices, as well as in the developing consciousness of many in the new immigrant groups. Generally speaking, the racist continuum runs from white to black, from "civilized" whites to "uncivilized" blacks, from high intelligence to low intelligence, from privilege and desirability to lack of privilege and undesirability. . . .

New non-European groups are customarily placed some-where along this continuum in relation to white emotions, racist thought, and discriminatory practice. On occasion, some Americans of color are placed toward the privileged white end of the racial spectrum. In the old apartheid system of South Africa some Asians were officially categorized as "honorary whites" because the white government needed Asian investors. In the U.S. case some Latinos and Asian Americans have from time to time been classified as "honorary whites" or "near whites" for somewhat similar reasons, such as in white-led, anti-affirmative-action efforts where Asian Americans are praised as being the equals of whites who supposedly need no affirmative action. Moreover, Frank Wu has accented the op-posite phenomenon in which some people of color are defined as "constructive blacks," as being near or at the black end of the racist continuum. . . . Moreover, at some points in history some Latino, Asian, and Native American groups may be moved to intermediate positions on the racist continuum—again princi-pally by white elites and for white purposes.

> *Often the lighter a group is, and the more Anglicized it seems to whites, the better it will be treated and viewed.*

Of course, all racially defined groups do not share the same fate or have the same experiences. The treatment of Americans of color has varied according to their time of entry, size, culture, physical characteristics, and wealth. In the case of Asian and Latino groups, . . . whites added a new dimension to the place-ment equation, that of "foreignness." Yet in every case it is the *dominant white group* that has set the major terms for their in-corporation and interpretation. For instance, one important study of early California history shows that Mexican, Asian, Na-tive, and African American groups did not develop in exactly the same way in California history, yet each was shaped by the preexisting framework of white supremacy, the central organiz-ing principle of U.S. society that was brought there by white mi-grants from the East. Those migrating to the West carried the system of U.S. racism with them—in their heads, hearts, practices, and institutions. They brought a well-developed ideology rationalizing black subordination and applied these ideas, often with new embellishments, to other groups seen as intellectually or culturally inferior. . . .

For later groups of non-European immigrants, whites' racist attitudes and practices targeting them were tailored to the particular conditions of these entrants. These groups have been shaped dramatically in this tailoring process. When, for instance, Asian American or Latino groups have become important for whites seeking their labor, whites have often ranked and categorized them along the light-to-dark, and close/not close to European-American culture, continua. Often the lighter a group is, and the more Anglicized it seems to whites, the better it will be treated and viewed. Thus, if light-skinned Cuban Americans are defined by whites as "near to white," they will have a different experience than darker-skinned immigrants of color, including darker Latinos like most Mexican Americans, whom many whites will place toward the "black end" of the socioracial continuum. . . .

Recently, certain groups among Latino Americans, such as lighter-skinned, middle-class Cuban Americans and South Americans, and certain groups among Asian Americans, such as middle-class Indian, Chinese, and Japanese Americans, have frequently been accepted as closer to the white than the black end of the racist continuum. However, this near-white placement is not ordinarily extended to the majorities of the largest Latino groups—Mexican Americans and Puerto Ricans.

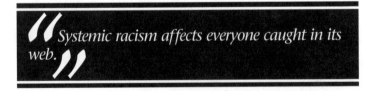

Systemic racism affects everyone caught in its web.

Whites make much use of placement in the intermediate status in order to keep the racist system flexible but intact. For example, when white commentators and analysts write or say positive things about the success of certain Asian or Latino American groups, they usually single out those who are lighter skinned and white acting. They point to the achievements of groups like middle-class Japanese Americans, Asian-Indian Americans, or Cuban Americans to suggest that Asian and Latino Americans are working harder and assimilating better to the core culture than black Americans. White often cite some in these groups as examples of achievement without a need for affirmative action. In this way the racist system is protected and reproduced, as one group is placed or played off against another to white advantage. . . .

Continuing discrimination today

An intermediate status on the white-to-black continuum also does not mean equality in rights, perquisites, and privileges with whites. Today, there is still much stereotyping and discrimination—including violently racist attacks—directed at intermediate groups, with the most attacks seemingly being directed at their darker skinned members. . . .

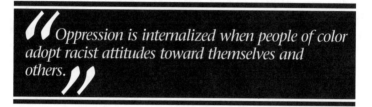

Oppression is internalized when people of color adopt racist attitudes toward themselves and others.

White attacks on Latinos and Asian Americans often take the form of racially motivated hate crimes, some of which are violent. For example, one report for Orange County in California reported 169 hate crimes there in just 1998, a number up from the previous year. While blacks were the most frequent targets, both Latino and Asian Americans were singled out for a variety of hate crimes. Today, across the nation, hundreds of racially motivated crimes against Latinos and Asian Americans are reported each year, with many others going unreported. These hate crimes have ranged from racist graffiti making threats of violence—often painted on homes or businesses or circulated on the Internet—to violent attacks, such as the racially motivated killing of a Vietnamese American student in California. . . .

Many Latinos and Asian Americans have felt pressured to give up their real identities in order to be as white as they can be. . . .

Yet the effects of this conformity to whiteness on them and their children have often been negative, with significant numbers facing great personal distress, painful self-blame, physical or mental illness, or alcoholism and drug addiction. Some have committed suicide as a result of pressures ultimately grounded in white racism. Today, there is often much pressure on Asian American youth to assimilate to whiteness that comes from the media and peer groups, especially in white majority suburbs, as well as from parents or other relatives. . . .

Hostility among subordinated griefs: links to white racism

Systemic racism affects everyone caught in its web. It is the social context for relations between all Americans, those defined as white and those defined as nonwhite. Intermediate groups often come to stereotype or attack those below them on the racial ladder, who may in turn retaliate, and these *internecine* [mutually destructive] attacks reinforce the racist system set in place by and for whites. Historically, whites have encouraged groups below them on the status ladder to stereotype and disparage each other. Stereotypes and prejudices in one racially subordinated group that target those in other subordinated groups are not independent of the larger context of systemic racism. Many negative racial images carried in subordinated communities exist because of the age-old racist ideology originally created by whites to rationalize white-on-black oppression. All groups of color assimilate many of the attitudes of the dominant society. As the black legal scholar Charles Lawrence has put it, "we use the white man's words to demean ourselves and to disassociate ourselves from our sisters and brothers. And then we turn this self-hate on other racial groups who share with us the ignominy of not being white." Many other scholars of color have also noted the ways in which oppression is internalized when people of color adopt racist attitudes toward themselves and others.

The white supremacist system intentionally fosters hostility between groups of color. When those higher on the white racist ladder express racist views about those lower, this helps preserve the systemic racism that benefits whites the most. By asserting that one's own group, though subordinated, is still better than those considered lower, members of an in-between group underwrite the racist ladder of privilege. Intergroup stereotyping and hostility among communities of color are very useful for whites who can play down the significance of their own racist thinking and practice. Whites can assert that "everyone is prejudiced."

Racist attitudes and images are central to the operation of systemic racism. What most Americans know about racial and ethnic matters beyond their own experience is what they are taught by those who control major avenues of socialization, such as the movies, music videos, television, radio, and print media that circulate racist images not only in the United States but across the globe. When these stereotyped images and accompanying discriminatory propensities are brought by Asian, Latino, and other immigrants to the United States, they can become the basis for intergroup conflict. These attitudes and practices are not independent, but generated by the now global white-racist order. Much negativity between groups of color reflects the foundation of systemic racism. . . .

Conclusion

For nearly four centuries those whose stolen labor has been central to the development of prosperity and wealth for white Americans—black Americans—are those who have most required control, segregation, and discrimination. As a group, black Americans are the most American in blended ancestry and are among the most American in the amount of time (nearly four centuries) spent working to build the prosperity of the new nation, yet they are also among the *least* American historically in terms of their rights, privileges, and opportunities. The oppression endured by black Americans is much more than a mental construction in white heads. Their oppressive reality is one that has been economically, physically, socially, and ideologically constructed.

Social science research on torture has found that people can endure much if there appears to be some hope of escape from such severe conditions, but torture is much harder to endure when it has gone on for some time and those tortured feel there is no hope of escaping. Drawing on this insight, one can perhaps understand why African Americans often have a different sense of how burdensome, omnipresent, and imbedded is the system of racist oppression than do other Americans, including many other Americans of color. Today as in the past, black Americans must operate with collective memories of many generations of racist oppression with its well-developed antiblack ideology. As a group they have an amplified culture of resistance that has enabled them to endure and counter this racist torture for centuries. Fifteen generations of oppression create a deep, critical, and nuanced perspective that may be different from that developed over one or two generations of racial discrimination. . . . The majorities in most Asian and Latino American groups are recent immigrants and their children. Some researchers suggest that compared with native-born black Americans many of these immigrants are less aware of or downplay the discrimination they face, in part because they are trying to establish an economic toehold and in part because they compare their current situation with that of the home country, and by this latter standard the United States often looks good.

However, it seems likely that as the next U.S.-born generations of Latinos and Asian Americans come of political age the barriers and pain of systemic racism will be attacked more openly, and many more will likely come to share the views of black Americans about organizing to bring major changes in the racist system. Historically, in the organized pursuit of civil rights and equality in the United States black Americans have usually led the way. Since at least the early 1900s they have forced the passage of all major civil rights laws and the majority of the pivotal executive orders and court decisions protecting or extending antidiscrimination efforts. Latinos, Native Americans, and Asian Americans have been able to make some use of these civil rights mechanisms to fight discrimination against their own groups, and this will likely continue in the future.

2

Race Relations in the United States Are Remarkably Good

Abigail Thernstrom,
interviewed by Charlotte Hays

Abigail Thernstrom is a senior fellow at the Manhattan Institute in New York, a member of the Massachusetts State Board of Education, and a commissioner on the U.S. Commission on Civil Rights. She and her husband, Harvard historian Stephan Thernstrom, are the coauthors of America in Black and White: One Nation, Indivisible.

Although the mainstream media continue to trumpet the evils of widespread racism in America, in truth, race relations have improved dramatically. More than ever, blacks are climbing into the middle and upper classes and have confidence in the level of opportunity available to them. Obviously, problems still exist, but the Democratic Party and liberal media are too quick to scream racism at every opportunity. For example, they blame racially biased testing for underachieving urban schools, rather than the ineffective administrators and teachers who run those schools. Likewise, there were definite problems with Florida's recount during the 2000 presidential election, but none of them were racially motivated. Continuing to portray blacks as a victimized race in America may help the Democrats win future elections, but it is not an honest portrayal of contemporary race relations.

Abigail Thernstrom, interviewed by Charlotte Hays, "What Nobody Wants to Say About Race: Author and Civil Rights Commissioner Abigail Thernstrom Talks to Charlotte Hays," *Women's Quarterly*, Autumn 2001. Copyright © 2001 by the Independent Women's Forum, www.iwf.org. Reproduced by permission.

[The *Women's Quarterly*]: Diane McWhorter, author of *Carry Me Home, Birmingham, Alabama,* . . . had a [July 2001] piece about Birmingham in the *New York Times Magazine*. It was about the trial of the last defendant in the 1963 bombing of the Birmingham church that killed four little girls. McWhorter seemed to be saying that, despite the outward civility, little had changed in Birmingham since the bombing. What do you make of this effort to deny real progress in racial matters?

THERNSTROM: The picture has changed radically, and it is time to acknowledge that fact. McWhorter is clearly becoming one of the darlings of the moment in the mainstream media, and I have liked some of her writings in the past. But she is profoundly wrong on this question. It is time for the *New York Times* and the chattering classes in general to wake up and celebrate how far we have come. Their message to whites seems to be: It's 10:00 A.M., and it's time for your daily five minutes of guilt. The mainstream media celebrate the voices of pessimists.

The Washington Post . . . did some polling on racial attitudes and analyzed the results. In reporting on the poll, the *Post* essentially said, whites are in a state of deep denial; they don't see the radical racial inequality around them. In fact, the actual poll suggests even more confidence in the level of opportunity in American society on the part of blacks than whites. Sixty-one percent of blacks, but only 46 percent of whites, said they believed their children would enjoy a higher standard of living than they did.

TWQ: In *America in Black and White*, you and your husband [Harvard historian Stephan Thernstrom] quote the journalist Brent Staples. When Staples was in the process of being hired by the *New York Times*, he said his editor wanted to know if he was "a faux Chevy Chase [Maryland] Negro or an authentic nigger," who had grown up "poor in the ghetto, besieged by crime and violence." There is a tendency for white intellectuals to insist that blacks be hostile.

THERNSTROM: That's true, but becoming less so, which is a sign of progress. I see a dawning recognition of the diversity within the group that we call "the black community," which is not a "community," given the diversity of black experience today. There is an increasing recognition of social class differences and of differences in political values among blacks, although the divisions are not yet reflected in election results.

TWQ: In your book, you point out that there was such improvement in test scores among black children between 1980 and 1988 that, had this rate of improvement continued, African-Americans and whites would now have the same test scores. What happened?

THERNSTROM: Nobody knows what happened to stop the progress, which doesn't, in fact, matter. We don't need to know the root causes of a problem in order to try and attack it. In the case of education, we know what good schools look like. But how to put them in place across the country? That's the tough question. The entire public education system is stacked against real change.

TWQ: What do good schools look like? Often the children who most need education to better their lot in life, including blacks, get the worst schools.

The mainstream media celebrate the voices of pessimists.

THERNSTROM: Urban black students, particularly, get an education that is inadequate to their needs. Some wonderful schools are serving them very well, however. They are just few and far between. They all look more or less the same. They are highly disciplined. They offer an often-needed structure to these children's lives. They concentrate on the core subjects—reading and math, mainly. The hours are very long. The school year is very long. The teaching is superb. There is great leadership at the top of the school. And the principal is an instructional leader for all of the teachers. The students read serious literature. And they aren't allowed to wallow in victimization. The teachers deliver a very strong "no excuses" message, even though many of these kids do have a genuinely lousy life. But the teachers don't care what else is going on in their lives; they still have to learn their times tables because when they're thirty, nobody is going to ask whether life in their neighborhood was a bummer.

TWQ: What about the attack on testing as racially biased?

THERNSTROM: The tests aren't racially biased. These children need the skills that the good tests assess. These tests give us information that we need.

TWQ: As you point out in the book, many African-Americans believe that there is lingering racism and that they need the federal government to protect them. That seems to be key to a lot of what happens in politics.

THERNSTROM: There are good historical reasons why blacks feel so vulnerable without the protective arm of the federal government. It was, after all, the federal government that really broke the back of the Jim Crow South. Federal courts intervened with judicial decisions that insisted upon racial equality. Federal legislation changed the status of blacks almost overnight. But the era of dependence on the federal government should be over. And today, many government regulations are, in fact, impediments to black progress. Government is the problem, nor the solution. For instance, the regulatory maze in a city like Chicago is an obstacle course for inexperienced would-be entrepreneurs, many of whom are black and Hispanic. The Institute for Justice has long been attacking this problem; it has been representing blacks and Hispanics whose private sector dreams are thwarted by public sector rules.

TWQ: The African-American vote is essential to the Democratic Party. Neither [Jimmy] Carter nor [Bill] Clinton would have been president without it. I sometimes wonder if some of the bitterness that is injected into politics is just a form of demagoguery [impassioned appeals to the prejudices and emotions of the populace], an effort to hold onto this group of voters.

There is a tendency for white intellectuals to insist that blacks be hostile.

THERNSTROM: Sure, but the Democrats don't have a monopoly when it comes to demagoguery which is endemic in politics. Such demagoguery, however, is particularly destructive on the issue of race. The Democratic Party keeps ratcheting up the sense, on the part of blacks, that they are victims, that the deck is stacked against them. And thus we have a racially defined group in America whose members feel angry and alienated—who feel that this country is not their country. And that's a danger to the fragile fabric of American politics and society.

TWQ: Let's talk about the U.S. Civil Rights Commission on which you now serve. Tell me about its involvement in the recount in Florida [during the 2000 presidential election], and the hearings that were held and your role in the hearings.

THERNSTROM: The commission held three days of hearings in Florida. And it heard countless witnesses. The bottom line for me: The election was far from perfect in Florida, which was undoubtedly true in other states as well. But, race per se, racial discrimination per se, played absolutely no part in the outcome. And that, of course, runs counter to the commission's report. Its central finding was that blacks were nine times more likely than whites—and I'm putting it in a passive voice deliberately because the commission's report puts it in a passive voice—to find that their ballots had been spoiled. The implication was that somehow [Florida governor] Jeb Bush and [former Florida secretary of state] Katherine Harris figured out which ballots were cast by black voters and managed to crumple them up. Or mutilate them in some way. . . .

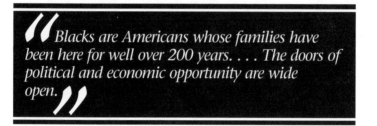

Blacks are Americans whose families have been here for well over 200 years. . . . The doors of political and economic opportunity are wide open.

TWQ: Was there any real evidence that blacks were prevented from voting in Florida?

THERNSTROM: No. There was some evidence that some poll workers were not very helpful to any voters (regardless of race or ethnicity), and there were stories of confusion and jammed phone lines. Perhaps most compelling of all was the evidence of insufficient accommodations for the disabled. But none of these problems had anything to do with race. In fact, there was a witness in Florida who said she had problems with poll workers. I said to her, "Look, it sounds to me as if you had difficulties at the polls, which you shouldn't have had. But it doesn't look to me as if it had anything to do with race." And she said, "Race? Who was talking about race? These were black poll workers." So yes, there were problems. And the state of Florida has taken steps to remedy them. Was there anything distinctive about the problems in that state? I don't think so, but nobody else has put any other state under a microscope, either now or in previous elections. . . .

TWQ: I am going to ask a cynical question. As I said, African-Americans are an important constituency to the Democratic Party. Could the commission's report on Florida's voting be pure demagoguery?

THERNSTROM: Absolutely. . . . The majority on the commission were determined to paint George W. Bush as an illegitimate president. And that's what the Florida report was all about. And they clearly wanted to send a message to black voters that Bush is not their president and that the Republican Party is not their party. It's a dangerous message. The commission seems determined to reinforce the belief on the part of too many blacks that they are a separate nation within our nation, outsiders to the American experiment. In fact, precisely the opposite message should be delivered. Blacks are Americans whose families have been here for well over 200 years. They have shaped American culture in a myriad of important and wonderful ways. And the doors of political and economic opportunity are wide open.

3

Racism Undermines the U.S. Judicial System

Paul Street

Paul Street is director of research at the Chicago Urban League. His articles, essays, and reviews have appeared in In These Times, Z Magazine, Monthly Review, *the* Journal of Social History, Mid-America, *and the* Journal of American Ethnic History.

The civil rights movement may have successfully eliminated overt demonstrations of public bigotry, but racism lives on in America's courts and prison system. By unfairly targeting and imprisoning black men, the country is ripping apart the social fabric of black communities and transferring the earning potential of those men to white towns that profit from the construction and administration of massive prison complexes. The result is a modern-day slavery of sorts, with white America benefiting from keeping black men in shackles and black America limited politically and economically. Upon release from prisons, ex-cons have a difficult time finding work, have been hardened by prison life, and often resort to illegal activities to earn a living. Whites then use this vicious cycle as proof of blacks' inability to succeed and general inferiority.

Defined simply as overt public bigotry, racism in the United States has fallen to an all-time low. Understood in socioeconomic, political and institutional terms, however, American racism is as alive as ever. More than thirty years after the heroic victories of the civil rights movement, Stanley Aronowitz [a professor of sociology at the City University of New York] notes, "the stigma of race remains the unmeltable condition of the black social and economic situation." Consider a *Chicago Tribune* article that appeared well off the front page, under the title "Towns Put Dreams in Prisons." In downstate Hoopeston, Illinois, there is "talk of the mothballed canneries that once made this a boom town and whether any of that bustling spirit might return if the Illinois Department of Corrections comes to town." Seeking jobs and economic growth, Hoopeston's leaders are negotiating with state officials for the right to host a shiny new maximum-security correctional facility. "You don't like to think about incarceration," Hoopeston's Mayor is quoted as saying, "but this is an opportunity for Hoopeston. We've been plagued by plant closings." The mayor's judgment is seconded in the *Tribune*'s account of the considerable benefits, including dramatically increased tax revenues, that flowed to Ina, Illinois, after it signed up to become a prison town a few years ago.

Two things are missing from this story. The first is an appropriate sense of horror at the spectacle of a society in which local officials are reduced to lobbying for prisons as their best chance for economic growth. The second concerns the matter of race. Nowhere did the reporter or his informants (insofar as they are fully and accurately recorded) mention either the predominantly white composition of the keepers or the predominantly black composition of the kept in the prison towns that increasingly look to the mass incarceration boom as the solution to their economic problems. As everyone knows, but few like to discuss, the mostly white residents of those towns are building their economic "dreams" on the transport and lockdown of unfree African-Americans from impoverished inner-city neighborhoods in places like Chicago, Rockford, East St. Louis, and Rock Island.

The new racism: America's prison system

This second absence is consistent with the politically correct rules of the new racism that plagues the United States at the turn of the millennium. There is a widespread belief among whites—deeply and ironically reinforced by the demise of open public racial prejudice—that African-Americans now enjoy equal and color-blind opportunity. "As white America sees it," write Leonard Steinhorn and Barbara Diggs-Brown in their sobering "By the Color of Their Skin: The Illusion of Integration and the Reality of Race," "Every effort has been made to welcome blacks into the American mainstream, and now they're on their own. . . . 'We got the message, we made the corrections—get on with it.'" "Going Downstate" Corrections, indeed. Nowhere, perhaps, is the persistence and even resurgence of racism more evident than in America's burgeoning "correctional" system. At the start of the twenty-first century, blacks are 12.3 percent of U.S. population, but they make up fully half of the roughly two million Americans currently behind bars. On any given day, 30 percent of African-American males ages 20 to 29 are "under correctional supervision"—either in jail or prison or on probation or parole. And according to a chilling statistical model used by the Bureau of Justice Statistics, a young black man age sixteen in 1996 faces a 29 percent chance of spending time in prison during his life. The corresponding statistic for white men in the same age group is 4 percent. The remarkable number and percentage of persons locked up by the state or otherwise under the watchful eye of criminal justice authorities in the United States—far beyond those of the rest of the industrialized world—is black to an extraordinary degree.

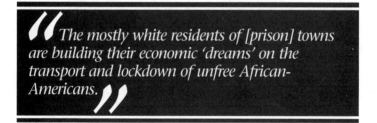

The mostly white residents of [prison] towns are building their economic 'dreams' on the transport and lockdown of unfree African-Americans.

This harsh reality gives rise to extreme racial dichotomies. Take, for example, the different meanings of the phrase "going downstate" for youths of different skin colors in the Chicago metropolitan area. For many white teens, those words evoke the image of a trip with Mom and Dad to begin academic careers at the prestigious University of Illinois at Urbana-Champaign or at one of the state's many other public universities. But for younger Chicago-area blacks, especially males (just 6 percent of the state's prisoners are female), "going downstate" more likely connotes a trip under armed guard to begin prison careers at one of the state's numerous maximum- or medium-security prisons. Indeed, Illinois has 149,525 more persons enrolled in its four-year public universities than in its prisons. When it comes to blacks, who make up 12.25 percent of the public university population, it has 5,500 more prisoners, making blacks

66 percent of the state's prisoners. For every African-American enrolled in those universities, at least two are in prison or on parole in Illinois.

Similar differences of meaning can be found in other states with significant black populations. In New York, where the relevant phrase is "going upstate," the Justice Policy Institute and the Correctional Association of New York report that in the 1990s more blacks entered prison just for drug offenses than graduated from the state's massive university system with undergraduate, masters, and doctoral degrees combined. In some inner-city neighborhoods, researchers and advocates report, a preponderant majority of black males now possess criminal records. Criminologists Dina Rose and Todd Clear have found black neighborhoods in Tallahassee, Florida, where every resident can identify at least one friend or relative who has been incarcerated. In many predominantly black urban communities across the country, it appears, incarceration is so widespread and commonplace that it has become what the U.S. Bureau of Justice Statistics director Jan Chaiken recently called "almost a normative life experience." Boys are growing up with the sense that it is standard for older brothers, uncles, fathers, cousins, and, perhaps, someday, themselves to be locked up by the state.

Labor market disenfranchisement

Researchers and advocates tracking the impact of mass incarceration find devastating consequences in high-poverty black communities. The most well known is the widespread political disenfranchisement of felons and ex-felons. The economic effects are equally significant. African-Americans are disproportionately and often deeply disenfranchised in competitive job markets by low skills, poor schools, weakened family structures, racial discrimination in hiring and promotion, and geographic isolation from the leading sectors of job growth. When prison and felony records are thrown into that mixture, the results can be disastrous. It is not uncommon to hear academic researchers and service providers cite unemployment rates as high as 50 percent for people with criminal records. One study, based in California during the early 1990s, found that just 21 percent of that state's parolees were working full time. In a detailed study, Karen Needels found that less than 40 percent of 1,176 men released from Georgia's prison system in 1976 had any officially recorded earnings in each year from 1983 to

1991. For those with earnings, average annual wages were exceedingly low and differed significantly by race: white former inmates averaged $7,880 per year and blacks made $4,762. In the most widely cited study in the growing literature on the labor market consequences of racially disparate criminal justice policies, Harvard economist Richard Freeman used data from the National Longitudinal Survey of Youth (NLSY). Limiting his sample to out-of-school men and controlling for numerous variables (drug usage, education, region, and age) that might bias upward the link between criminal records and weak labor market attachment, Freeman found that those who had been in jail or on probation in 1980 had a 19 percent higher chance of being unemployed in 1988 than those with no involvement in the criminal justice system. He also found that prison records reduced the amount of time employed after release by 25 percent to 30 percent.

More recently, Princeton sociologist Bruce Western mined NLSY data to show that incarceration has "large and enduring effects on job-prospects of ex-convicts." He found that the negative labor market effects of youth incarceration can last for more than a decade and that adult incarceration reduces paid employment by five to ten weeks annually. Because incarceration rates are especially high among those with the least power in the labor market (young and unskilled minority men), the U.S. justice system exacerbates inequality.

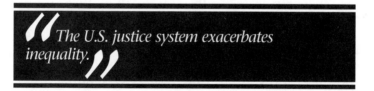

The U.S. justice system exacerbates inequality.

This research is consistent with numerous experimental studies suggesting that the employment prospects of job applicants with criminal records are far worse than the chances of persons who have never been convicted or imprisoned. It is consistent also with evidence from labor market intermediaries dealing with ex-offenders. Project STRIVE, an established job-placement program that mainly serves younger minority males in inner-city Chicago, reports that it placed thirty-seven of fifty ex-offenders in jobs [in 2001], leaving a 26 percent unemployment rate even for people who went through an especially successful program. The Center for Employment Opportunity in New York

City is another "successful" program. Focused specifically on ex-offenders, it fails to place nearly a third of its clients. Another standard bearer in the field, "Project Rio" of the Texas Workforce Commission, claims to process fifteen thousand inmates a year. After one year, a little over two-thirds of parolees who go through Project Rio hold jobs. More telling, since most ex-offenders are thrown into the labor market without the benefit of a transitional employment program, just 36 percent of a group of Texas parolees who did not enroll in Project Rio had a job one year after their release. And "even when paroled inmates are able to find jobs," the *New York Times* reported [in the fall of 2001], "they earn only half as much as people of the same social and economic background who have not been incarcerated."

The obstacles to ex-offender employment include the refusal of many employers even to consider hiring an "ex-con." Employers routinely check for criminal backgrounds in numerous sectors, including banking, security, financial services, law, education, and health care. But for many jobs, employer attitudes are irrelevant: state codes place steep barriers to the hiring of ex-offenders in numerous government and other occupations. At the same time, Western notes, "the increasingly violent and overcrowded state of prisons and jails is likely to produce certain attitudes, mannerisms, and behavioral practices that 'on the inside' function to enhance survival but are not compatible with success in the conventional job market." The alternately aggressive and sullen posture that prevails behind bars is deadly in a job market where entry-level occupations increasingly demand "soft" skills related to selling and customer service. In this as in countless other ways, the inmate may be removed, at least temporarily (see below), from prison, but prison lives on within the ex-offender, limiting his or her freedom on the outside.

A vicious circle

The situation arising from mass black incarceration is fraught with self-fulfilling policy ironies. At the very moment that American public discourse in racial matters has become officially inclusive, the United States is filling its expanding number of cellblocks with an ever-rising sea of black people monitored by predominantly white overseers. Echoes of slavery haunt the new incarceration state, reminding us of unresolved historical issues in the United States of Amnesia.

Mass incarceration is just as ironically juxtaposed to welfare reform. Even as the broader political and policy-making community is replacing taxpayer-financed "welfare dependency" with "workforce attachment" and free market discipline leading (supposedly) to "self-sufficiency" and two-parent family stability among the urban "underclass," criminal justice policies are pushing hundreds of thousands of already disadvantaged and impoverished blacks further from minimally remunerative engagement with the labor market. It does this by warehousing them in expensive, publicly financed, sex-segregated holding pens, where rehabilitation has been discredited and authoritarian incapacitation is the rule.

> **❝** *Echoes of slavery haunt the new incarceration state, reminding us of unresolved historical issues in the United States of Amnesia.* **❞**

Droves of alienated men are removed from contact with children, parents, spouses, and lovers, contributing to the chronic shortage of suitable male marriage partners and resident fathers in the black community. Black humor on Chicago's South Side quips that "the only thing prison cures is heterosexuality." A connection probably exists between rampant sexual assault and sexual segregation behind prison bars and the disturbing fact that AIDS is now the leading cause of death among blacks between the ages of 25 and 44. Incarceration deepens a job-skill deficit that is a leading factor explaining "criminal" behavior among disadvantaged people in the first place. "Crime rates are inversely related," Richard B. Freeman and Jeffrey Fagan have shown, "to expected legal wages, particularly among young males with limited job skills or prospects." The "war on drugs" that contributes so strongly to minority incarceration also inflates the price of underground substances. Combined with ex-offenders' shortage of marketable skills in the legal economy, it creates irresistible incentives for the sort of income-generating conduct that leads back to prison. The lost potential earnings, savings, consumer demand, and human and social capital that result from mass incarceration cost black communities untold millions of dollars in potential economic development, worsening an inner-city political economy already crippled by decades of capital flight and de-industrialization. The dazed and embittered graduates of the prison-industrial complex are released back into a small number of predominantly black and high-poverty ZIP codes and census tracts, deepening the concentration of poverty, crime, and despair that is the hallmark of modern American "hyper-segregation" by race and class.

Meanwhile, prisoners' deletion from official U.S. unemployment statistics contributes to excessively rosy perceptions of American socioeconomic performance that worsen the political climate for minorities. Bruce Western has shown that factoring incarceration into unemployment rates challenges the conventional American notion that unregulated labor markets have been out-performing Europe's supposedly hyper-regulated employment system. Far from taking a laissez-faire approach, "the U.S. state has made a large and coercive intervention into the labor market through the expansion of the legal system." An American unemployment rate adjusted for imprisonment would rise by two points, bringing the U.S. ratio much closer to that of European nations, where including inmates raises the joblessness rate by only a few tenths of a percentage point. Counting prisoners would raise the official black male unemployment rate, which Western estimates at nearly 39 percent during the mid-1990s (including prisoners). Western and his colleague Becky Petit find that, when incarceration is factored in, there was "no enduring recovery in the employment of young black high-school drop-outs" during the eight-year Clinton employment boom.

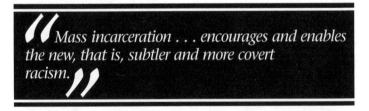

Mass incarceration . . . encourages and enables the new, that is, subtler and more covert racism.

By artificially reducing both aggregate and racially specific unemployment rates, mass incarceration makes it easier for the majority culture to continue to ignore the urban ghettoes that live on beneath official rhetoric about "opportunity" being generated by "free markets." It encourages and enables the new, that is, subtler and more covert racism. Relying heavily on longstanding American opportunity myths and standard class ideology, this new racism blames inner-city minorities for their own "failure" to match white performance in a supposedly now free, meritorious, and color-blind society. Whites who believe that racial barriers have been lifted in the United States think that people of color who do not "succeed" fall short because of choices they made or because of inherent cultural or even biological limitations.

Correctional Keynesianism

The ultimate policy irony at the heart of America's passion for prisons can be summarized by the phrase "correctional Keynesianism" [after economist John Maynard Keynes]: the prison construction boom fed by the rising market of black offenders is a job and tax-base creator for predominantly white communities that are generally far removed from urban minority concentrations. These communities, often recently hollowed out by the de-industrializing and family-farm-destroying gales of the "free market" system, have become part of a prison-industrial lobby that presses for harsher sentences and tougher laws, seeking to protect and expand their economic base even as crime rates continue to fall. They do so with good reason. The prison-building boom serves as what British sociologist David Ladipo calls "a latter-day Keynesian infrastructural investment program for [often] blight-struck communities. . . . Indeed, it has been phenomenally successful in terms of creating relatively secure, decent paid, and often unionized jobs."

According to Todd Clear, the negative labor market effects of mass incarceration on black communities are probably minor "compared to the economic relocation of resources" from black to white communities that mass incarceration entails. As Clear explains,

> Each prisoner represents an economic asset that has been removed from that community and placed elsewhere. As an economic being, the person would spend money at or near his or her area of residence—typically, an inner city. Imprisonment displaces that economic activity: Instead of buying snacks in a local deli, the prisoner makes those purchases in a prison commissary. The removal may represent a loss of economic value to the home community, but it is a boon to the prison [host] community. Each prisoner represents as

much as $25,000 in income for the community in which the prison is located, not to mention the value of constructing the prison facility in the first place. This can be a massive transfer of value: A young male worth a few thousand dollars of support to children and local purchases is transformed into a $25,000 financial asset to a rural prison community. The economy of the rural community is artificially amplified, the local city economy artificially deflated. It's a disturbing picture, even in this cynical age, full of unsettling parallels and living links to chattel slavery: young black men being involuntarily removed as "economic assets" from black communities to distant rural destinations where they are kept under lock and key by white-majority overseers. It is difficult to imagine a more pathetic denouement to America's long, interwoven narratives of class and racial privilege. The rise of correctional Keynesianism is one of the negative and racially charged consequences of technically color-blind political-economic processes. . . .

Conclusion

To be sure, it is no simple matter to determine the precise extent to which mass incarceration is simply exacerbating the deep socioeconomic and related cultural and political traumas that already plague inner-city communities and help explain disproportionate black "criminality," arrest, and incarceration in the first place. Still, it is undeniable that the rush to incarcerate is having a profoundly negative effect on black communities. Equally undeniable is the fact that black incarceration rates reflect deep racial bias in the criminal justice system and the broader society. Do the cheerleaders of "get tough" crime and sentencing policy really believe that African-Americans deserve to suffer so disproportionately at the hands of the criminal justice system? There is a vast literature showing that structural, institutional, and cultural racism and severe segregation by race and class are leading causes of inner-city crime. Another considerable body of literature shows that blacks are victims of racial bias at every level of the criminal justice system—from stop, frisk, and arrest to prosecution, sentencing, release, and execution. These disparities give legitimacy to the movement of ex-offender groups for the expungement of criminal and prison records for many nonviolent offenses, especially in cases where ex-convicts have shown an earnest desire to go straight.

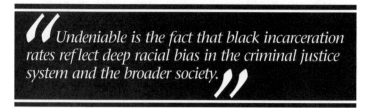

Undeniable is the fact that black incarceration rates reflect deep racial bias in the criminal justice system and the broader society.

Further and deeper remedies are required. These include a moratorium on new prison construction (to stop the insidious, self-replicating expansion of the prison-industrial complex), the repeal of laws that deny voting rights to felons and ex-felons; amnesty and release for most inmates convicted of non-violent crimes; decriminalization of narcotics; the repeal of the "war on drugs" at home and abroad; revision of state and federal sentencing and local "zero tolerance" practices and ordinances; abolition of racial, ethnic and class profiling in police practice; and the outlawing of private, for-profit prisons and other economic activities that derive investment gain from mass incarceration. Activists and policy makers should call for a criminal- to social-justice peace dividend: the large-scale transfer of funds spent on mass arrest, surveillance and incarceration into such policy areas as drug treatment, job-training, transitional services for ex-offenders and public education regarding the employment potential of ex-offenders. They should call for the diversion of criminal justice resources from crime in the streets (that is, the harassment and imprisonment of lower-class and inner-city people) to serious engagement with under-sentenced crime in the suites. More broadly, they should seek a general redistribution of resources from privileged and often fantastically wealthy persons to those most penalized from birth by America's inherited class and race privilege. America's expanding prison, probation and parole populations are recruited especially from what leading slavery reparations advocate Randall Robinson calls "the millions of African-Americans bottom-mired in urban hells by the savage time-release social debilitations of American slavery."

The ultimate solutions lie, perhaps, beyond the parameters of the existing political economic order. "Capitalism," Eugene Debs argued in 1920, "needs and must have the prison to protect itself from the [lower-class] criminals it has created." But the examples of Western Europe and Canada, where policy makers prefer prevention and rehabilitation through more social democratic approaches, show that mass incarceration is hardly an inevitable product of capitalism. And nothing can excuse policy makers and activists from the responsibility to end racist criminal justice practices that significantly exacerbate the difficulties faced by the nation's most disadvantaged. More than merely a symptom of the tangled mess of problems that create, sustain and deepen America's insidious patterns of class and race inequality, mass incarceration has become a central part of the mess. For these and other reasons, it will be an especially worthy target for creative democratic protest and policy formation in the new millennium.

4

Environmental Racism Is a Major Problem

U.S. Commission on Civil Rights

The U.S. Commission on Civil Rights is an independent, bipartisan agency of the executive branch. It was established in 1957 to study and collect information relating to discrimination or denial of equal protection of the laws under the Constitution because of race, color, religion, sex, age, disability, or national origin, or in the administration of justice.

The United States has a history of environmental racism. Lacking social, economic, and political power, minority communities across the country have had little influence in zoning and land-use decisions. Consequently, these communities have been taken advantage of and unfairly saddled with polluting facilities such as landfills and toxic dumps. Proponents of these projects claim that they create jobs and an opportunity for community growth, but the reality has been a declining quality of life and ongoing health problems. Conditions have improved somewhat since President Bill Clinton signed an executive order in 1994 mandating that federal agencies incorporate environmental justice into their work and programs, but widespread environmental justice remains an illusion.

Environmental justice [according to Environmental Protection Agency (EPA) administrator Christine Todd Whitman], is the "fair treatment of people of all races, income, and cultures with respect to the development, implementation and enforcement of environmental laws, regulations, and policies, and their

U.S. Commission on Civil Rights, "Not in My Backyard: Executive Order 12,898 and Title VI as Tools for Achieving Environmental Justice," September 4, 2003.

37

meaningful involvement in the decision-making processes of the government." The first environmental justice cases were brought in 1979 in Texas and in 1982 in North Carolina. In 1979, residents of Northwood Manor in East Houston alleged that the decision to place a garbage dump in their neighborhood was racially motivated in violation of their civil rights under § 1983 of the Civil Rights Act. The district court in *Bean* [*v. Southwestern Waste Management Corp.*] found that the placement of the dump would irreparably harm the community. The court specifically found that the landfill would "affect the entire nature of the community, its land values, its tax base, its aesthetics, the health and safety of its inhabitants, and the operation of Smiley High School, located only 1700 feet from the site." Unable to establish intentional discrimination with sufficiently particularized statistical data showing a pattern or practice of placing waste facilities in communities of color, and unable to provide the court sufficiently detailed factual information on the siting decision, the residents were not granted relief and the plant was built. The case, however, launched the use of the courts as a tool for the new movement and highlighted the need for data collection and access to information by communities challenging environmental decisions.

> *Zoning practices allowing heavy industry in poor communities and communities of color contribute to the overall decline of these communities.*

In 1982, African Americans in Afton, Warren County, North Carolina, protested a decision to place a highly toxic Polychlorinated biphenyls (PCBs) landfill in their community and captured national attention. Those protesting the landfill argued that the mostly African American community was selected because it was minority and poor. At the time, Afton was 84 percent African American and Warren County was one of the poorest in North Carolina. In fact, as reported by Dr. Robert Bullard in *Dumping in Dixie*, the Afton PCB landfill site was not "scientifically the most suitable" site, because the water table was a mere 5–10 feet below the surface and the risk of groundwater contamination was high.

It was during this time in the late 1970s and early 1980s that many low-income communities and communities of color across the country, including Latinos, African Americans, Asian Americans, and Native Americans, concluded that unequal social, economic, and political power relationships made them more vulnerable to health and environmental threats than the society at large. More than 10 years after these early efforts in Texas and North Carolina, race continues to play a significant role in decisions concerning the location of polluting facilities such as landfills and toxic dumps. EPA [director Barry Hill] points to at least "76–80 studies that have consistently said that minorities and low-income communities are disproportionately exposed to environmental harms and risks." A 1983 General Accounting Office (GAO) study, *Siting Hazardous Waste Landfills and Their Correlation with Racial and Economic Status of Surrounding Communities*, was one of the first studies to focus on the distribution of environmental risks. This study confirmed what environmental justice advocates believed, that racial minorities are burdened with a disproportionate amount of environmental risks. The report also confirmed that income was a factor in siting hazardous and toxic facilities. In other studies exploring the roles of both race and income, race was determined to be the stronger predictor of exposure to environmental hazards.

> *Immigrant groups, the poor, African Americans and other people of color, and industry are often excluded from white and affluent communities.*

Four years after the GAO report, a more comprehensive national study by the Commission for Racial Justice of the United Church of Christ, *Toxic Wastes and Race in the United States: A National Report on the Racial and Socioeconomic Characteristics of Communities with Hazardous Waste Sites*, confirmed that race and ethnicity were the most significant factors in deciding where to place waste facilities, landfills, and other environmental hazards. In 1994, the follow-up report, *Toxic Wastes and Race Revisited*, found that the disproportionate environmental burden placed on communities of color had, in fact, grown since the 1987 report. The 1994 report found that "people of color were 47 percent more likely than whites to live near a commercial hazardous waste facility" and that between 1980 and 1993 the concentration of people of color living in areas with commercial hazardous waste facilities increased 6 percent, from 25 to 31 percent. A study by Evan Ringquist, *Equity and Distribution of Environmental Risk: The Case of TRI Facilities*, concluded that racial bias exists in the distribution and density of Toxic Release Inventory (TRI) facilities, with African Americans and Hispanics exposed to the highest levels of risk. In 2001, Manuel Pastor, Jr., and Jim Sadd concluded that "the bulk of the research does seem to point to disproportionate exposure to hazards in minority communities."

The role of zoning and development in environmental racism

Housing segregation, the influence of race in local zoning practices, and infrastructure development all contribute to this disparity. Federal agencies, notably the Federal Housing Authority and the Veterans Administration, had practices that supported or fostered housing segregation. These practices included subsidizing suburban growth at the expense of urban areas, supporting racial covenants by denying African Americans mortgage insurance in integrated communities, providing mortgage insurance in segregated residential areas, and redlining.

Zoning practices and decisions that, on their face are race neutral, routinely allow communities of color and poor communities to be zoned "industrial" and significantly contribute to the disproportionate placement of hazardous and toxic industries in these neighborhoods. It has been established that areas zoned industrial have a greater environmental burden and health risks than areas only zoned for residential use. Therefore, zoning practices allowing heavy industry in poor communities and communities of color contribute to the overall decline of these communities. As the presence of industry increases, property values decrease, community members are slowly displaced, and these areas become increasingly undesirable. The spiraling decline in property values makes locating industry in these areas increasingly more attractive. The remaining residents, usually the poor and people of color, have no other housing alternatives and little political clout. Without political influence, these communities are not able to prevent siting and permitting decisions that have adverse environmental and health consequences. In short, these communities are not able to mount the "NIMBY" or "not in my backyard" defense.

A July 2003 report by the National Academy of Public Administration (NAPA), *Addressing Community Concerns: How Environmental Justice Relates to Land Use Planning and Zoning*, citing the work of Juliana Maantay, reported that historical and current local land-use and zoning policies are "a root enabling cause of disproportionate burdens [and] environmental injustice." The NAPA report also concurred with the conclusion put forth by Yale Rabin, that zoning and land-use decisions are often based on considerations of race and are powerful legal weapons "deployed in the cause of racism" by allowing certain undesirables to be excluded from areas. As a result, immigrant groups, the poor, African Americans and other people of color, and industry are often excluded from white and affluent communities. Local zoning and land-use decisions, however, need not only be a tool for racism or the creation of disparate impact. An awareness and careful consideration of the distributional issues, or disparities in the distribution of environmental benefits and burdens, during the local zoning and land-use process would help address the disparate environmental and health impact on communities of color and poor communities. Including representatives from affected communities on local planning and zoning boards and commissions may facilitate this awareness. NAPA reported that the most recent survey on the composition of planning commissions found that:

- Most planning and zoning board members are men.
- More than nine out of 10 members are white.
- Most members are 40 years old or older.
- Boards contain mostly professionals and few, if any, non-professional or community representatives.

While zoning and planning are state and local concerns, federal agencies could assist in reducing the disparities resulting from zoning and land-use policies by requiring local land-use authorities to incorporate and implement the concept of environmental justice in the zoning and land-use policies as a prerequisite for receiving federal funding. NAPA supports this approach.

While many point to racial segregation in housing and race-conscious land-use and zoning policies as factors contributing to disparities in the distribution of environmental burdens, others explain the disparities by examining market forces. A "market dynamics" interpretation seeks to account for the disproportionate number of hazardous and toxic facilities in communities of color and poorer communities by establishing that these communities developed after the hazardous and toxic industrial facilities were established. According to the theory, these populations intentionally decide to live near hazardous and toxic sites as a result of market forces, specifically, cheap housing and the possibility of jobs. A study by Manuel Pastor on disproportionate siting versus "minority move-in" in Los Angles County, however, linked siting dates with addresses of toxic storage and disposal facilities to a database tracking changes in socioeconomic variables from 1970 to 1990. The study determined that areas scheduled to receive these facilities were mostly low-income, minority, and disproportionately composed of renters; after the facilities arrived, there was no significant increase in the minority population. It appears, therefore, that minorities attract toxic storage and disposal facilities but these facilities do not attract minorities.

Luke Cole and Shelia Foster, in *From the Ground Up: Environmental Racism and the Rise of the Environmental Justice Movement*, found "inconclusive empirical support to date for the 'market dynamics' explanation for racial or economic disparities in the distribution of hazardous facilities." As also noted by Cole, proponents of the market dynamics explanation acknowledge that racial discrimination influences market forces by limiting housing options for African Americans and other people of color through discrimination in renting, redlining, zoning practices, and the discriminatory enforcement of environmental laws and regulations.

Communities affected by environmental decision making

Whether based solely on race or on market dynamics influenced by race, minority communities in Cuyahoga County, Ohio; Jefferson County, Texas; Chester, Pennsylvania; and Macon, Bibb County, Georgia, live in some of the most polluted communities in the United States. In Ohio, for example, the top four polluters in Cleveland are all located in or adjacent to minority communities. Cleveland Laminating Corporation is located in a predominately minority community in Cuyahoga County; within one mile of the plant 90 percent of the population is minority. This plant is the third worst air polluter in the county and is in the top 10 percent in the country for releasing carcinogens into the air.

Jefferson County, Texas, ranks in the top 10 percent for the worst air quality in the country. Over 240,000 people in Jefferson County face a cancer risk more than 100 times the goal set by the Clean Air Act. Seventy-two percent of the air cancer risk is from mobile sources such as cars and other vehicles, and 24 percent is from major industrial facilities such as chemical plants, steel mills, oil refineries, power plants, and hazardous waste incinerators.

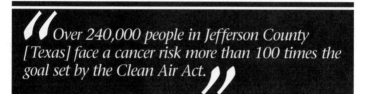

Over 240,000 people in Jefferson County [Texas] face a cancer risk more than 100 times the goal set by the Clean Air Act.

In 2000, based on toxic chemical releases from manufacturing facilities, this county ranked among the "dirtiest/worst 10% of all counties in the U.S. in terms of air releases of recognized reproductive toxicants," [as reported by environmental watchdog organization Scorecard]. Chemicals with "reproductive toxicity" are chemicals resulting in adverse effects on the male or female reproductive systems. Reproductive toxicity may include changes in sexual behavior, decreased fertility, or increased miscarriages. Potential sources of land contamination in the county include three Superfund sites, and in 2000, this county ranked among the "dirtiest/worst 20%" of all counties in the United States in underground injection. Underground injection is a method of land disposal in which liquid wastes are injected into known geological formations. The two major cities in Jefferson County, Beaumont and Port Arthur, are predominately minority and suffer most from these hazardous exposures. Beaumont, with a population of slightly more than 113,000, is 45.8 percent African American and 7.9 percent Hispanic; while Port Arthur, with 57,755 residents, is 43.7 percent African American and 17.5 percent Hispanic. Clark Refining and Marketing, Inc., in Port Arthur, and Mobile Oil Corporation, in Beaumont, each ranked in the worst 10 percent in the country for criteria air pollutant emissions in 1999. . . .

Chester, in Delaware County, Pennsylvania, is home to approximately 36,000 residents and one of the largest collections of waste facilities in the country. Seventy-five percent of Chester residents are African American as are 95 percent of residents in neighborhoods closest to the facilities. The poverty rate is 27.2 percent, three times the national average.

Bibb County, Georgia, has a population of 153,887; 47.3 percent of the population is African American, 50.1 percent white, 1.1 percent Asian, 1.3 percent Hispanic, and 0.2 Native American. However, Macon, Georgia, in Bibb County, has a population that is 62 percent African American. Only 32 percent of the city's residents have a high school diploma or GED, and 25 percent live below the poverty level.

Air quality problems are related to the operation of two Georgia Power Company coal-fired power plants, Plant Scherer and Plant Bowen near Macon. Another plant, Plant Arkwright, in Macon, contributes to the poor air quality. In 2000, it ranked in the worst 20 percent in the country for total environmental releases of major chemicals and wastes. In 1999, the Arkwright plant was among the worst 10 percent in the country for nitrogen oxide emissions and in the worst 20 percent for sulfur dioxide emissions.

> *Low-income residents and people of color are disproportionately exposed to a variety of environmental toxins in their respective neighborhoods, schools, homes, or workplaces.*

Also in Macon are Riverwood International and Brown & Williamson Tobacco. A 1999 criteria air pollutant emissions report of Riverwood International found that the plant was among the worst 10 percent in the country for carbon monoxide, nitrogen oxides, particulate matter, and volatile organic compounds. Volatile organic compounds are defined as chemicals that participate in the formation of ground ozone; ozone is a respiratory toxicant and a significant contributor to smog. The 2000 rankings of major chemical releases or wastes placed Riverwood International in the worst 10 percent in the country in total environmental releases and in air releases of recognized carcinogens.

A 1999 criteria air pollutant emissions report ranked Brown & Williamson better than Riverwood International and Plant Arkwright in air pollutant emissions in Macon for the same period. Brown & Williamson, however, did have higher than average carbon monoxide, nitrogen oxide, and sulfur dioxide emissions. The 2000 rankings for major chemical releases or waste at this facility placed it in the worst 20 percent in the country for total environmental releases and air releases of recognized developmental toxicants.

> *African American children suffer from lead poisoning at rates twice that of white children at every income level.*

There are other examples. In 2002, it was disclosed that for nearly 40 years, in the rural, poor, and minority community of Anniston, Alabama, the Monsanto Corporation, while producing the now-banned industrial coolants known as PCBs at a local factory, routinely discharged toxic waste into a west Anniston creek and dumped millions of pounds of PCBs into open-pit landfills. EPA and the World Health Organization classify PCBs as "probable carcinogens." [Michael Grunwald of the *Washington Post*] reported that "thousands of pages of Monsanto documents—many emblazoned with warnings such as 'Confidential: Read and Destroy'"—proved that the company intentionally concealed what it was doing and what it knew about the illegal dumping.

Increasingly throughout the nation, low-income residents and people of color are disproportionately exposed to a variety of environmental toxins in their respective neighborhoods, schools, homes, or workplaces. For example, a 1995 Washington State health survey indicated that in South Seattle, communities of color and those neighborhoods with a significant number of low-income residents house more industrial and waste facilities than other parts of the state. The report found that in several South Seattle neighborhoods, industrial facilities are next door to homes. In South Park, one Seattle neighborhood, [reporter Larry Lange wrote,] "more than 40 industrial and waste facilities are situated within a one to five-mile radius of residential homes."

Native American reservations have been consistently exposed to hazardous chemicals. Reservations have also become prime locations for solid waste landfills, military weapons testing, and nuclear storage facilities. In fact, [wrote Robert Bullard, director of the Environmental Justice Resource Center,] "more than 35 Indian reservations were targeted for landfills, incinerators and radioactive waste facilities in the early 1990's."

This may explain why Native Americans experience some of the worst pollution in the United States. Exposure to the waste facilities, landfills, lead-based paint, and other pollutants has an adverse impact on human health. Communities housing these facilities report increased rates of asthma, cancer, delayed cognitive development, and other illnesses.

Adverse health impact

Due in significant part to substandard air quality, asthma is emerging as an epidemic among people of color in the United States. A Centers for Disease Control (CDC) report on asthma rates in 2000–2001 found that African Americans were 4 percent more likely to have been diagnosed with asthma than whites and that African Americans have an asthma death rate 200 percent higher that whites. The CDC reports in its *National Asthma Control Program: Improving Quality of Life and Reducing Costs 2003* that "rates of severe asthma continue to disproportionately affect poor, minority, inner city populations."

Lead-based paint exposure and poisoning is a particular problem for poor children and families. For example, 35 percent of families with incomes of less than $30,000 live in housing with lead hazards. Compare this figure to that for families with incomes above $30,000; only 19 percent of these families live in housing with lead hazards. According to the CDC:

> Childhood lead poisoning remains a major preventable environmental health problem in the United States. About half a million children younger than 6 years of age in the United States have blood lead levels of at least 10 micrograms per deciliter (µg/dL), a level high enough to adversely affect their intelligence, behavior and development. Minority and poor children are disproportionately affected.

African American children suffer from lead poisoning at rates twice that of white children at every income level, but for low-income African American children the rate is 28.4 percent compared with 9.8 percent for low-income whites. According to researchers, this disparity is directly related to African Americans' disproportionately residing in older homes because of racial segregation in housing.

The lead abatement programs of EPA and HUD [the Department of Housing and Urban Development] are central to combating lead poisoning, which is often found in older housing and low-income housing units. Housing built before 1960 is five to eight times more likely to have lead hazards than housing built between 1960 and 1978. Lead is also found in soil and is related to the deterioration of exterior paints containing lead. The economic and age factors discussed in relation to lead-based paint prevalence in housing also hold true for bare soil lead hazards. The CDC supports consideration of health issues in decisions about housing and the environment. Such considerations are imperative if severe adverse health issues related to excessive lead-based paint exposure are to be eliminated. As noted previously, reduced intelligence, impaired hearing, reduced stature, and many other adverse health effects are linked to lead exposure.

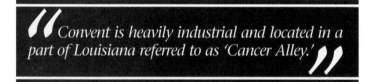

Convent is heavily industrial and located in a part of Louisiana referred to as 'Cancer Alley.'

Many communities are exposed to multiple pollutants and toxins. Federal agencies, however, have not adopted formal cumulative impact standards to assess the risk to human health from exposures from multiple chemicals from multiple sources, even though Executive Order 12,898 requires consideration of multiple and cumulative exposures. Additionally, there is no presumption that multiple exposures, in any amount, constitute an adverse health impact. EPA released its *Framework for Cumulative Risk Assessment* in May 2003, calling it a "basis for future guidance" on cumulative risk assessments. The report does not create a protocol for assessing the health impact of multiple exposures. This "piling-on" of exposures should be given great weight when assessing the health risk associated with placing yet another facility in a neighborhood. Also a concern is the absence of a methodology or formal framework for conducting a cumulative risk assessment that considers social, economic, cultural, and behavioral factors that increase health risks.

The Executive Order requires that "human health research, whenever practicable and appropriate, shall include diverse segments of the population in epidemiological and clinical studies, including segments at high risk from environmental hazards, such as minority populations [and] low-income populations." According to community groups and advocates, agencies have been slow in incorporating these groups into studies and research.

Finally, § 3-302 of the order requires federal agencies to collect, analyze, and maintain data assessing whether programs and activities have resulted in a disproportionately high and adverse health impact on low-income and minority communities. This requires agencies to collect data on environmental and human health risks borne by populations identified by race, national origin, and income.

Environmental racism or economic opportunity?

Despite the demonstrated health risks, locating waste and toxic facilities in low-income and minority neighborhoods is viewed, by some, as a welcome means of providing these communities economic opportunities. Supporters of the economic benefit theory point to the experiences of Select Steel and Shintech, Inc., as examples. Both facilities relocated from minority communities after environmental justice challenges were raised.

Select Steel promised to provide jobs in the economically disadvantaged community of Genesee County, Michigan. Community members, however, were concerned about the adverse health effects created by the Select Steel facility. Their protests, and challenges to the granting of a permit to Select Steel, forced the facility to relocate.

Similar events occurred in Louisiana involving Shintech's proposal to locate a plastics plant near Convent. Company officials estimated that the facility would generate 2,000 temporary construction jobs and 165 permanent jobs in the predominately African American community with high unemployment. Convent is heavily industrial and located in a part of Louisiana referred to as "Cancer Alley," an 80-mile area along the Mississippi River between Baton Rouge and New Orleans with a heavy concentration of oil refineries and petrochemical plants. This area accounts for approximately one-fourth of the country's petrochemical pollution. Because of health concerns, the community protested the presence of the Shintech plant and, eventually, the plant located elsewhere.

Many community and environmental advocates disagree that jobs are being created for the communities exposed to the greatest health risks. Chemical plants and others facilities, they note, do not hire local residents. The St. Lawrence Cement Plant, in South Camden, New Jersey, occupied 12 acres of waterfront property and cost $50 million to build. However, it created only 16 jobs, eight for the nearby neighborhood. Of the 1,878 permanent jobs created by the 10 chemical plants in St. Gabriel, Iberville Parish, Louisiana, only 6.7 percent or 164 jobs went to local residents, and these chemical plants employed only 20 African Americans from the local area.

Additionally, the data reflects that when better paying, skilled jobs are created they often require skills not present in the workers from the immediate community. St. James Parish, where Shintech sought to locate its Convent plant, has an African American population of approximately 10,300 or half of the total population of the Parish. Of this population there were only 17 qualified engineering technicians, 19 science technicians, and 20 qualified computer equipment operators. Chemical plants that located in St. James Parish did not have access to local workers with the skills they required. In the Convent area, only 58 percent of the population completed high school, and the Louisiana Chemical Association reported that the low educational level in the area impeded Shintech from hiring local residents. As a result of the lack of skilled workers, skilled and higher paying jobs are filled by commuters living in the surrounding suburbs.

> *Communities are concerned that they are being forced to choose between their health and the hope of economic opportunity.*

For the jobs that are created, local residents are not given the right of first refusal or guaranteed access to training to prepare them for available jobs. In fact, EPA lacks legal authority to ensure that members of affected communities qualify for jobs created by a siting or permitting decision, and does not have authority to condition approval of state programs on their hiring practices. EPA does not maintain records of which state regulatory bodies condition permits on specific hiring practices, or the reasons for such conditions if they are imposed by the states.

Communities are concerned that they are being forced to choose between their health and the hope of economic opportunity. According to Bullard, . . . these families are not able to relocate to escape the hazards because racism, housing discrimination, and residential segregation "force many people of color to have to live next door to facilities. Racism has made it very difficult for many communities and many residents to exit environmentally threatening conditions." There appears to be governmental support for policies that would continue to disproportionately place polluting industries in minority and poor communities to stimulate development. According to Michael Steinberg, an attorney with the law firm of Morgan, Lewis & Bockius, and head of the Environmental Practice Group, the emphasis should not be on "distributional issues," but on using Brownfields redevelopment programs to clean up after facilities have shutdown:

> And I would say not only do we not want to prohibit it. We have on the books, and indeed, the President is signing today a new law designed to encourage, to attract, to induce jobs, businesses, and industry into communities that are economically blighted, that are in need of redevelopment. Often environmental cleanup is the first step on the path to redevelopment, but federal and state governments around the country are pushing to bring jobs to these communities. And so to say that we're going to shut the door because of concerns about distributional issues I think is really totally contrary to that policy.

The Brownfields Revitalization and Environmental Restoration Act of 2001, signed by President George W. Bush in January 2002, is laudable in that it seeks to bring economic development to areas by cleaning up abandoned, contaminated sites and redeveloping them for commercial or residential use A 1992 evaluation by the *National Law Journal*, however, found glaring inequities in EPA's cleanup enforcement efforts. According to the authors, "there is a racial divide in the way the U.S. government cleans up toxic waste sites and punishes polluters. White communities see faster action, better results and stiffer penalties than communities where blacks, Hispanics, and other minorities live. These conditions exist whether the community is wealthy or poor." The same problems exist 10 years after this report.

In addition to uneven cleanup, Brownfields programs do not always result in beneficial reuse of properties in minority and poor communities due to lax enforcement of existing regulations, as described in the *National Law Journal* report and noted by environmental advocates. For example, the opening of a Home Depot as a part of a Brownfields project in Harlem created 400 part-time jobs. Unfortunately, in addition to the jobs, the community experienced a significant increase in truck traffic and related emissions in an area with one of the highest asthma rates in the country. Some cities with Brownfields redevelopment projects seek to use the reclaimed properties for industrial purposes, potentially increasing pollution and exposure to environmental hazards. Other cities, however, seek mixed-use activity and non-polluting businesses. Community advocates support and encourage "clean" industry such as schools, colleges and universities, and financial institutions.

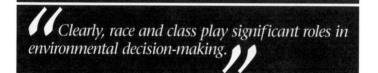

Clearly, race and class play significant roles in environmental decision-making.

Even with these concerns about its fair enforcement and implementation, Brownfields redevelopment remains an important and necessary environmental and economic tool as noted by some advocates and in a December 2001 report by the U.S. Conference of Mayors. The report credits Brownfields redevelopment projects with revitalizing neighborhoods, increasing city tax bases, and improving the environment. However, Brownfields cannot fully address the health and quality of life issues in the environmental justice context. Assisting local governments in identifying and attracting "clean" industry, instead of industrial plants or certain types of commercial activity, would be a significant step toward improving the usefulness of the Brownfield program. Ensuring equal enforcement and implementation of environmental regulations, . . . as well as providing sufficient funding so that the progress of the cleanup efforts is not slowed, would aid in restoration of these communities. . . .

Conclusion

Clearly, race and class play significant roles in environmental decision-making, with low-income communities and communities of color being disproportionately affected by siting decisions and the permitting of facilities. Siting and permitting are not, however, the sole sources of environmental concerns in these communities. Exposure to lead-based paint, diesel emissions, noise, odor, and other pollutants also diminishes the health of these communities. . . .

There should be a review of the administration of the Superfund program to ensure that all communities receive prompt attention and that sites in communities of color receive the same level and quality of decontamination as cleanup sites in white and affluent communities. . . .

Federal agencies should require state and local zoning and land-use authorities, as a condition for receiving and continuing to receive federal funding, to incorporate and implement the principles of environmental justice into their zoning and land-use policies.

5

The Problem of Environmental Racism Has Been Exaggerated

Jim F. Couch, Peter M. Williams, Jon Halvorson, and Keith Malone

Jim F. Couch is a professor of economics at the University of North Alabama in Florence. Peter M. Williams is an assistant professor of economics at the University of North Alabama in Florence. Jon Halvorson is an assistant professor of economics at Indiana University of Pennsylvania. Keith Malone is a graduate student in economics at the University of Alabama in Tuscaloosa.

Since charges of environmental racism became widespread in the 1980s, the issue has been the subject of careful study. Research does not support the claim that industrial polluters and waste dumps are located in minority communities with racist motivation. Rather, studies theorize that existing areas of high industrial pollution attract minorities who seek job opportunities and cheap housing. Furthermore, some studies find minority populations are not exposed to higher levels of pollutions even when hazardous-waste sites are near. Moreover, by discouraging "unhealthy" industrials from building in the state, Mississippi is unfairly limiting employment opportunities for its minority citizens.

Jim F. Couch, Peter M. Williams, Jon Halvorson, and Keith Malone, "Of Racism and Rubbish: The Geography of Race and Pollution in Mississippi," *The Independent Review*, vol. 8, Fall 2003, pp. 235–47. Copyright © 2003 by The Independent Institute, 100 Swan Way, Oakland, CA 94021-1428 USA, www.independent.org. Reproduced by permission.

> Nobody can question that, for far too long, communities across this country—low income, minority communities—have been asked to bear a disproportionate share of our modern industrial life.
> —EPA Administrator Carol Browner,
> April 22, 1994 (Earth Day)

The notion of racism has recently taken a new twist. Using demographic variables in the description of hazardous-waste sites, the United Church of Christ Commission on Racial Justice (1987) reported a correlation between race and the location of waste-producing facilities. Charges of environmental racism and environmental injustice quickly followed. Robert D. Bullard asserts: "Environmental discrimination is defined as a disparate treatment of a group or community based on race, class, or some other distinguishing characteristic. White racism is a factor in the impoverishment of black communities and has made it easier for black residential areas to become dumping grounds for all types of health-threatening toxins and industrial pollution."

Anecdotal evidence [supporting] this proposition certainly exists. The area around Baton Rouge, Louisiana, and extending south along the Mississippi River—an area of high minority population—has been called "cancer alley" or the "toxic corridor." Likewise, the so-called Devil's Swamp, one of Louisiana's largest hazardous-waste dump sites, is located near the low-income, high-minority population of Scotlandville.

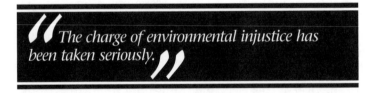

The charge of environmental injustice has been taken seriously.

The charge of environmental injustice has been taken seriously. At least two national conferences have been held to review the existing research on the subject and to propose policies to alleviate the problem. The [Bill] Clinton administration took steps to outlaw environmental discrimination. A 1994 executive order instructed all federal agencies to be on the lookout for evidence of such discrimination. In 1998, the Environmental Protection Agency (EPA) was instructed to investigate facilities whose emissions have a disparate impact on minorities. Any state agency that approves such facilities is to be found in violation of Title VI of the Civil Rights Act of 1964.

In this article, we add to the growing literature investigating the link between environmental waste and both minorities and the poor. We consider data on pollutants emitted in the state of Mississippi. The next section provides a brief description of externalities and an overview of the benefits and costs of government intervention. Next we provide a review of the existing pertinent literature, then present pollution and racial-demographic data, and follow that with a conclusion and final comments.

Residents should have the right to choose

In the case of pollution, third-party residents suffer from the emissions, but the market ignores their suffering. Government can seek to correct the externality by regulating the activity or by applying a tax on the polluter, the revenue from which can be transferred to the residents who bear the pollution burden.

[In "The Problem of Social Costs"] Ronald Coase advocates an alternative solution that calls for the harmed parties to negotiate with the polluter. The residents may be willing to "sell" some of their clean environment to the polluting firm. Although exposure to toxic chemicals is thought to be associated with a host of human health problems, residents may focus instead on the benefits of heavy industry. A recent example is worthy of consideration.

In 1997, Greenpeace and other political organizations blocked a Shintech factory from locating in St. James Parish, Louisiana, by making use of the EPA's Title VI rule forbidding new pollution sources in areas that have a greater minority representation than the rest of the state. The plastics plant ended up being located in another state in a predominantly white community. This shift occurred even though an overwhelming majority of the citizens of St. James Parish expressed a desire for the facility in a poll conducted by the local chapter of the National Association for the Advancement of Colored People (NAACP).

According to the proponents of environmental justice, minority residents' willingness to accept polluting plants serves only to illustrate the desperation of the poor: "Polluting industries exploit the pro-growth, pro-jobs sentiment exhibited among the poor . . . and minority communities. Industries such as paper mills . . . and chemical plants, searching for operation space, found these communities to be a logical choice for their expansion" [Bullard, "Dumping in Dixie: Race, Class, and Environmental Quality," 1994].

[In *Race and the Incidence of Environmental Hazards*] B. Bryant and P. Mohai contend, however, that rather than exploiting a desperation for jobs, companies target minority communities because such communities have less political clout and therefore represent the path of least resistance. Still, whatever one's views on job desperation or paths of least resistance, the question remains: Are minorities and the poor actually subject to greater exposure to hazardous waste from polluting plants?

Existing research

As D. Friedman points out [in "The Environmental Racism Hoax," *American Enterprise*] many believe that "environmental justice" initially became a topic of policy analysis in 1982, when efforts to block the movement of a hazardous-waste landfill into a predominantly minority-populated area of North Carolina were unsuccessful. The fight over this toxic landfill led to the involvement of various politicians and ultimately of the EPA. EPA involvement in the form of issue statements and guidelines was most likely the impetus for studies that sought to find evidence of environmental injustice. Although such evidence exists, A. Holmes, B.A. Slade, and L.B. Cowart caution [in "Are Minority Neighborhoods Exposed to More Environmental Hazards?" *Real Estate Review*] that much of it adduced thus far is advocacy based and should be viewed skeptically.

[In *Spatial Inequality and the Distribution of Industrial Toxic Releases*] G. Daniels and S. Friedman have provided a comprehensive review of the literature. In these studies, the most common unit of analysis for data is the county, the zip code area, the region, or the census tract. Some of the studies that examined the entire United States and found a positive correlation between minority population and pollution are the United Church of Christ 1987, Zimmerman 1993, Perlin and Setzer 1995, Been 1997, Brooks and Sethi 1997, Ringquist 1997, Hite 2000, and Allen 2001. The United Church of Christ study is one of the most widely cited empirical studies, and it concluded that race was a significant factor in determining the location of polluting facilities. On the other hand, in the first comprehensive study of toxic-waste facilities to use census-tract data, D.L. Anderton and colleagues did not find any nationally consistent correlation between minorities and pollution.

Other studies have not examined the nation as a whole,

but have focused instead on particular regions, states, or still smaller units of observation. The U.S. General Accounting Office (GAO) completed one of the first regional studies in 1983. It compiled data on four hazardous-waste facilities in EPA Region 4 [comprising the Southeast states of Alabama, Florida, Georgia, Kentucky, Mississippi, North Carolina, South Carolina, and Tennessee]. The study concluded that the population surrounding three of these facilities was predominantly black. Bryant and Mohai studied the demographic characteristics of populations surrounding commercial hazardous-waste facilities in a three-county area around Detroit. They concluded that race is a more important factor than income in the distribution of these facilities. L.M. Burke, J.T. Boer and J.L. Pastor, and Sadd and colleagues found a positive correlation between minorities and pollution in Los Angeles County and in the Los Angeles metro area. Studies of Ohio and Florida also yield a positive correlation. Neither M.J. Cohen nor Susan L. Cutter, D. Holm, and L. Clark found a relationship between minority population and pollution. Likewise, Holmes, Slade, and Cowart found that the racial composition of the area did not influence the geographic distribution of pollutants or polluting facilities in Birmingham, Alabama.

> *Additional research suggests that economic factors rather than race itself account for apparent environmental racism.*

Additional research suggests that economic factors rather than race itself account for apparent environmental racism. J. Mitchell, D.S.K. Thomas, and S. Cutter (1999) point out [in "Dumping in Dixie Revisited: The Evolution of Environmental Injustices in South Carolina," *Social Science Quarterly*] that merely finding a correlation between large minority communities and industrial pollution is not necessarily evidence of environmental injustice. Does the correlation arise because polluting industries target minorities in their site selection, or do existing industries attract minorities because of job opportunities and lower property values? The researchers conducted a longitudinal analysis of industry and racial demographics in the state of South Carolina and found that the industries came first. That is, when the industrial plants were first constructed, minorities were not present in disproportionate number. Over time, however, the process of migration caused those areas to have a greater proportion of minorities. Thus, where industries came first, as in South Carolina, the public-policy implications of a correlation between minorities and pollution are unclear.

[In "Testing for Environmental Racism: Prejudice, Profits, Political Power," *Journal of Policing Analysis and Management*] J.T. Hamilton tested three economic theories: pure discrimination in siting decisions; differences in the willingness to pay for environmental amenities based on income and education; and differences in the probability of communities to engage in collective action against the location of the polluting site. Hamilton concluded that in terms of the distribution of externalities, from 1987 to 1992 the zip code areas targeted for toxic-facility expansion had a higher percentage of nonwhite residents than the zip code areas without net expansions. He also concluded that differences in the probability of collective action helped explain the distribution of pollution across communities. T. Lambert and C. Boerner found that in the case of St. Louis and Houston, "to the degree that environmental disparities exist, it is economic factors—not siting discrimination—that are behind many claims of environmental racism". For example, toxic facilities initially located in white areas often become surrounded by minority residents who are attracted by falling housing prices.

Mississippi pollution and race

The study we report here is based on a single state. In studies of discrimination, we may find that different regions of the country exhibit different levels of discriminatory behavior. The reasons for these differences include, but are not limited to, the cultural history, the laws, and the minority makeup of the different regions. Because the proponents of environmental racism claim that minorities lack both the financial means and the political clout to resist the siting of a polluting plant, state-by-state analysis is needed to control for the differing political structures that exist across the states. Further, because of likely differences in the distribution of education, income, and cultural preferences between minority groups of different regions, the ability of minorities as a group to avoid living in polluting areas may differ from state to state.

Studies investigating the nation as a whole can produce misleading findings and interpretations. The large number of Midwestern rural counties with a small minority population and little industry creates bias in a coast-to-coast study. [In "Distribution of Industrial Air Emissions by Income and Race in the United States," *Environmental Science & Technology*] S.A. Perlin and R.W. Setzer issue this caveat: "an analysis looking only at the national picture will miss important information which may lead to erroneous conclusions". Although an unusually rich data set might allow the researcher to control for these differing conditions, such a data set does not exist.

> *Toxic facilities initially located in white areas often become surrounded by minority residents who are attracted by falling housing prices.*

Here we investigate the claims of environmental injustice by focusing on Mississippi. Bullard has asserted, "the entire Gulf Coast region, especially Mississippi, Alabama, Louisiana, and Texas, has been ravaged by 'lax regulations and unbridled production'". Therefore, Mississippi—a state with an unpleasant race-relations history—serves as an excellent test case.

Like previous researchers, we use proximity to a polluting industry as a proxy for exposure. Researchers must take care to match the geographic unit of observation with the etiology [origin] of diseases. Following Perlin and Setzer, we use the county as the unit of analysis. The pollution data we consider are allowable emissions by firm, obtained on a county-by-county basis from the Mississippi Department of Environmental Quality, Title 5: Operating Permit Program. Pollution is measured in this data set as tons per year. The permit amount considered is the maximum allowed for the period from September 1, 1995, to August 31, 1996. Although the actual pollution may differ from the allowable amount, a charge of discrimination could hardly be sustained because some plants chose to produce less pollution than allowed.

We used two measures of pollution: total air pollutants and hazardous air pollutants (HAPs), a subset of total air pollutants. HAPs constitute an especially nasty group of chemicals thought to be responsible for the most significant risk of disease. By comparing the geographic pattern of pollutant emissions by county to the racial makeup of each county, we can assess whether the claims of environmental injustice hold up for the state of Mississippi. . . .

Conclusion

Based on the foregoing analysis, we conclude that no positive association exists between heavy black population and large amounts of air pollution in the state of Mississippi. If anything, [our research] show[ed] less pollution in counties with higher black representation.

These results suggest, at least with regard to Mississippi, that charges of environmental racism are highly exaggerated. Daniels and Friedman point out that two types of counties tend to have low levels of pollution: poor counties with little economic activity and wealthy counties that derive their income primarily from non-industrial sources. Lower levels of economic activity may explain why, in investigations of Mississippi county data, blacks as a group appear to be less exposed to pollution than nonblack residents.

If lower levels of economic activity are driving these results, then blocking new industry may be counterproductive in seeking to improve the lives of those living in predominantly minority counties. In response to the St. James Parish Shintech controversy, the local president of the Black Chamber of Commerce said, "I'm trying to think of a policy that would be more effective in driving away entrepreneurs and jobs from economically disadvantaged areas—and I can't do it". Indeed, in April 2001, the St. James Parish Council applied for a grant to study why its unemployment rate is so high. Dale Hymel, the St. James Parish president, sees no need for such a study: "When an industry looks at St. James Parish, and they find out Shintech was run out of St. James, they don't even want to look at us any further".

The final determination of the best public policy depends on how much weight is given to the benefits of jobs as against the cost of pollution to the area. Whatever the weight given to a clean environment, Mississippi's pattern of county-level air pollution hardly supports the notion of environmental injustice.

6

Racial Profiling Unfairly Targets Minorities

Gene Callahan and William Anderson

Gene Callahan has written for Ideas on Liberty, National Review Online, *and* Slick Times. *His book* Economics for Real People *was published in 2001 by the Ludwig von Mises Institute. William Anderson is an assistant professor of economics at Frostburg State University in Maryland and an adjunct scholar at the Ludwig von Mises Institute.*

The roots of racial profiling can be traced back to America's war on drugs in the 1980s when police were encouraged to stop and search members of certain groups. Two decades later, although conservatives dismiss racial profiling as a myth and police departments have been forced to change some procedures, the practice continues. One explanation for its persistence is the current state of asset seizure laws. Police departments are allowed to seize the property of suspected drug dealers and have an incentive to do so because a large portion of that revenue flows back to the departments. As a potential moneymaker for police, racial profiling makes sense even in the face of some bad publicity. Until these seizure laws are changed, racial profiling will endure.

It is early in the morning, and the well-dressed young African-American man driving his Ford Explorer on I-75 sees the blue lights of the Georgia State Patrol car behind him. The officer pulls behind the sport utility vehicle and the young man's heart begins to sink.

He is on his way to Atlanta for a job interview. The stop, ostensibly for speeding, should not take long, he reasons, as the highway patrol officer walks cautiously toward the Explorer. But instead of simply asking for a driver's license and writing a speeding ticket, the trooper calls for backup. Another trooper soon arrives, his blue lights flashing as well.

The young man is told to leave his vehicle, as the troopers announce their intention to search it. "Hey, where did you get the money for something like this?" one trooper asks mockingly while he starts the process of going through every inch of the Explorer. Soon, an officer pulls off an inside door panel. More dismantling of the vehicle follows. They say they are looking for drugs, but in the end find nothing. After ticketing the driver for speeding, the two officers casually drive off. Sitting in his now-trashed SUV, the young man weeps in his anger and humiliation.

Unmotivated searches like this are daily occurrences on our nation's highways, and blacks and white liberals have been decrying the situation for several years. Many conservatives, on the other hand, dismiss such complaints as the exaggerations of hypersensitive minorities. Or they say that if traffic cops do in fact pull over and search the vehicles of African Americans disproportionately, then such "racial profiling" is an unfortunate but necessary component of modern crime fighting.

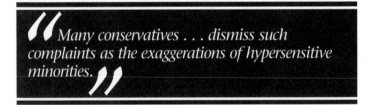

Many conservatives . . . dismiss such complaints as the exaggerations of hypersensitive minorities.

The incident described above should give pause to those who think that racial profiling is simply a bogus issue cooked up by black leaders such as Al Sharpton and Jesse Jackson to use as another publicity tool. One of us teaches in an MBA program that enrolls a fairly large number of African Americans, and the story comes from one of our students. Indeed, during class discussions, all of the black men and many of the black women told stories of having their late-model cars pulled over and searched for drugs.

While incidents of racial profiling are widely deplored today, there is little said about the actual root cause of the phenomenon. The standard explanations for racial profiling focus on institutional racism, but that idea runs contrary to the sea change in social attitudes that has taken place over the last four decades. On the contrary, the practice of racial profiling grows from a trio of very tangible sources, all attributable to the War on Drugs, that $37 billion annual effort on the part of local, state, and federal lawmakers and cops to stop the sale and use of "illicit" substances. The sources include the difficulty in policing victimless crimes in general and the resulting need for intrusive police techniques; the greater relevancy of this difficulty given the intensification of the drug war since the 1980s; and the additional incentive that asset forfeiture laws give police forces to seize money and property from suspects. Since the notion of scaling back, let alone stopping, the drug war is too controversial for most politicians to handle, it's hardly surprising that its role in racial profiling should go largely unacknowledged.

The practice of racial profiling

Although there is no single, universally accepted definition of "racial profiling," we're using the term to designate the practice of stopping and inspecting people who are passing through public places—such as drivers on public highways or pedestrians in airports or urban areas—where the reason for the stop is a statistical profile of the detainee's race or ethnicity.

The practice of racial profiling has been a prominent topic for the past several years. In his February [2001] address to Congress, President George W. Bush reported that he'd asked Attorney General John Ashcroft "to develop specific recommendations to end racial profiling. It's wrong, and we will end it in America." The nomination of former New Jersey Gov. Christine Todd Whitman as head of the Environmental Protection Agency was challenged on the basis of her alleged complicity in racial profiling practices in the Garden State. Whitman had pioneered her own unique form of "minority outreach" when she was photographed frisking a black crime suspect in 1996. Copies of the photo were circulated to senators prior to her confirmation vote. (By the same token, in February 1999, Whitman fired State Police Superintendent Carl A. Williams after he gave a newspaper interview in which he justified racial profiling and linked minority groups to drug trafficking.) More recently, Eleanor Holmes Norton, the District of Columbia's non-voting member of Congress, has tried to introduce legislation that would withhold federal highway dollars from states that have not explicitly banned racial profiling.

Although some observers claim that racial profiling doesn't exist, there is an abundance of stories and statistics that document the practice. One case where law enforcement officers were particularly bold in their declaration of intent involved U.S. Forest Service officers in California's Mendocino National Forest [in 2000]. In an attempt to stop marijuana growing, forest rangers were told to question all Hispanics whose cars were stopped, regardless of whether pot was actually found in their vehicles. Tim Crews, the publisher of the *Sacramento Valley Mirror*, a biweekly newspaper, published a memo he'd gotten from a federal law enforcement officer. The memo told park rangers "to develop probable cause for stop . . . if a vehicle stop is conducted and no marijuana is located and the vehicle has Hispanics inside, at a minimum we would like all individuals FI'd [field interrogated]." A spokeswoman for Mendocino National Forest called the directive an "unfortunate use of words."

Although some observers claim that racial profiling doesn't exist, there is an abundance of stories and statistics that document the practice.

The statistics are equally telling. Consider *Crises of the Anti-Drug Effort, 1999*, a report by Chad Thevenot of the Criminal Justice Policy Foundation, a group that monitors abuses of the American legal system. Thevenot writes: "76 percent of the motorists stopped along a 50-mile stretch of I-95 by Maryland's Special Traffic Interdiction Force (STIF) were black, according to an Associated Press computer analysis of car searches from January through September 1995. . . . Blacks constitute 25 percent of Maryland's population, and 20 percent of Marylanders with driver's licenses." As this story was being written, New Jersey was holding hearings on racial profiling, and one state police investigator testified that 94 percent of the motorists stopped in one town were minorities.

Minorities are not only more likely to be stopped than whites, but they are also often pressured to allow searches of their vehicles, and they are more likely to allow such searches. In March [2001], *The New York Times* reported that a 1997 investigation by New Jersey police of their own practices found that "turnpike drivers who agreed to have their cars searched by the state police were overwhelmingly black and Hispanic."

Some commentators, such as John Derbyshire in *National Review*, have defended racial profiling as nothing more than sensible police technique, where police employ the laws of probability to make the best use of their scarce resources in attacking crime. As Derbyshire put it in his February 19 [2001] story, "In Defense of Racial Profiling," the police engage in the practice for reasons of simple efficiency: "A policeman who concentrates a disproportionate amount of his limited time and resources on young black men is going to uncover far more crimes—and therefore be far more successful in his career—than one who biases his attention toward, say, middle-aged Asian women."

[Conservative columnist] George Will in an April 19 [2001] *Washington Post* column, contends that the use of race as a criterion in traffic stops is fine, as long as it is just "one factor among others in estimating criminal suspiciousness." Similarly, Jackson Toby, a professor of sociology at Rutgers, argued in a 1999 *Wall Street Journal* op-ed that, "If drug traffickers are disproportionately black or Hispanic, the police don't need to be racist to stop many minority motorists; they simply have to be efficient in targeting potential drug traffickers."

Clayton Searle, president of The International Narcotics Interdiction Association, writes in a report, *Profiling in Law Enforcement*, "Those who purport to be shocked that ethnic groups are overrepresented in the population arrested for drug courier activities must have been in a coma for the last twenty years. The fact is that ethnic groups control the majority of the drug trade in the United States. They also tend to hire as their underlings and couriers others of their same group." (Searle's report is available at www.inia.org/whats-new.htm#Profiling.)

Case probability vs. class probability

The stories and statistics that draw outrage tend to share two common elements: They involve a search for drugs and the prospect of asset forfeiture. These types of investigations have led police from the solid ground of "case probability" to the shifting sands of "class probability" in their quest for probable cause. Once police are operating on the basis of class probability, there is a strong claim that certain groups of people are being denied equal protection under the law.

Case probability describes situations where we comprehend some factors relevant to a *particular* event, but not all such factors. It is used when a doctor tells a patient, "Given your lifestyle, you'll probably be dead in five years." Class probability refers to situations where we know enough about a *class* of events to describe it using statistics, but nothing about a particular event other than the fact that it belongs to the class in question. Class probability is being used when an insurance company estimates that a man who is 40 today will probably live to be, on average, about 80. The insurance company is not making any statement about the particular circumstances of any particular man, but merely generalizing about the class of 40-year-old men.

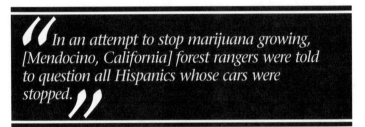

In an attempt to stop marijuana growing, [Mendocino, California] forest rangers were told to question all Hispanics whose cars were stopped.

This distinction helps us to differentiate two ways of using information about race or ethnicity in a police investigation. As an example of the first type, employing case probability, consider a mugging victim who has told the police that her mugger was a young Asian man. Here, it is quite understandable that the group of suspects investigated will not "look like America." There is no sense in forcing the police to drag in proportional numbers of whites, blacks, women, and so on, proving that they have interrogated a representative population sample of their city, before they can arrest an Asian fellow. No, their investigation should clearly focus on young Asian men.

It's not at all impossible that a prevalence of some type of criminal activity in some ethnic group will lead to many investigations that focus on members of that group. As long as this is based on evidence gathered from particular crimes, there is nothing untoward here. If it turns out, for instance, that Bulgarians are especially numerous among purse-snatchers in some city, then a summary of police interrogations might discover evidence of "Bulgarian profiling" in the investigation of purse-snatching. But this may be a statistical mirage if it turns out that no one in the police force set out to focus on Bulgarians as potential purse-snatchers. The emergent result is an unintended outcome of policemen following an entirely valid principle of crime investigation: Concentrate on suspects who fit the description you have of the suspect.

Racial profiling based on class probability

But when we turn our attention to the type of racial profiling that occurred on the highways of Maryland and New Jersey, or that is described in the Forest Service memo, we find a very different phenomenon, one where investigations proceeded on the basis of class probability. Here, before having evidence of a particular crime, police set out intending to investigate a high proportion of people of some particular race, ethnic group, age group, or so on. Their only justification is that by doing so, they increase their chances of discovering some crimes.

Additionally, there is a fundamental difference between the type of crime, such as the mugging example above, that is usually investigated by gathering evidence about a known crime, and narrowing the search based on such evidence, and the type investigated by looking in as many places as possible to see if one can find a crime. The first type of crime generally has a victim, and the police are aware of a specific crime that has been committed. The crime is brought to the attention of the police by a complainant, even if the complainant is a corpse.

> *Minorities are not only more likely to be stopped than whites, but they are also often pressured to allow searches of their vehicles.*

George Will in his defense of current police practice, points out: "Police have intelligence that in the Northeast drug-shipping corridor many traffickers are Jamaicans favoring Nissan Pathfinders." This is quite a different situation than having intelligence that a particular Jamaican robbed a store and escaped in a Pathfinder. If you are a law-abiding Jamaican who by chance owns a Pathfinder, you frequently will find yourself under police surveillance, even though the police have no evidence about any particular crime involving any particular Jamaican in a Pathfinder.

We could not have any effective law enforcement without allowing some scope for case probability. If your twin brother robs a bank in your hometown, it does not seem to be a civil rights issue if the police stop you on the street for questioning. When the police discover their mistake, they should apologize and make you whole for any damages you have suffered. Such an event, while unfortunate, is simply a byproduct of attempting to enforce laws in a world of error-prone human beings possessing less-than-perfect knowledge. It will be a rare event in law-abiding citizens' lives, and it is highly unlikely that such people will come to feel that they are being targeted.

However, the use of class probability in police investigations is correctly regarded with extreme suspicion, as it violates a basic principle of justice: The legal system should treat all citizens equally, until there is specific, credible evidence that they have committed a crime. In the cases we've been discussing, we can say that the odds that any particular young black or Hispanic man will be hassled by the police are much higher than for a white man who, aside from his race, is demographically indistinguishable from him. These minority men, no matter how law-abiding they are, know that they will be investigated by the police significantly more often than other citizens who are not members of their racial group. The social cost of the alienation produced by this situation cannot, of course, be measured, but common sense tells us that it must be great.

As important, in the majority of "crimes" that such stops discover, there is no third party whose rights have been violated, who can step forward and bring the crime to the attention of the police. To discover victimless crimes, investigators *must* become intrusive and simply poke around wherever they can, trying to see if they can uncover such a crime. When someone drives a few pounds of marijuana up I-95 from seller to buyer, who will come forward and complain? It's not merely that, as in the cases of robbery or murder, the perpetrator may try to hide his identity, but that the "crime" has no victim.

Drug war profiling practices

Both statistical studies and anecdotal evidence support the view that drug crimes are the almost exclusive focus of investigation in racial profiling cases. Hence, *The New York Times* reported in February [2001] that, "The New Jersey State Police said last week that the number of drug arrests on the Garden

State Parkway and the New Jersey Turnpike fell last year, after the department came under scrutiny for racial profiling. The number of drug charges resulting from stops on the turnpike were 370 [in 2000], compared with 494 drug charges in 1999. There were 1,269 charges filed in 1998. On the parkway, troopers reported 350 drug charges last year compared with 783 in 1999 and 1,279 in 1998."

> *The legal system should treat all citizens equally, until there is specific, credible evidence that they have committed a crime.*

The Record, a Bergen, New Jersey, newspaper, obtained state police documents [in the fall of 2000]. One document, used for training, teaches troopers to zero in on minorities when scanning state roadways for possible drug traffickers. Titled "Occupant Identifiers for a Possible Drug Courier," the document instructs troopers to look out for "Colombian males, Hispanic males, Hispanic and a black male together, Hispanic male and female posing as a couple." (One's mind boggles at how the police are able to detect that two Hispanics are "posing" as a couple as they zip by at 60 miles per hour.) The undated document also teaches troopers how to use supposed traffic violations, such as "speeding" and "failure to drive within a single lane," as a pretext to pull over suspected drug couriers.

If police have a goal of maximizing drug arrests, they may indeed find that they can achieve this most easily by focusing on minorities. Blacks on I-95 in Maryland, for instance, had a significantly higher initial propensity to carry drugs in the car than did whites. "Racial Bias in Motor Vehicle Searches: Theory and Evidence," a 1999 study by University of Pennsylvania professors John Knowles, Nicola Persico, and Petra Todd, shows that despite the fact that blacks were stopped three-and-a-half times more than whites, they were as likely to be carrying drugs. But this doesn't mean their propensity to carry is the same. If we assume that the high likelihood of being stopped reduces some blacks' willingness to carry drugs, then if not for the stops, they would have been carrying proportionally much more than whites. The Penn professors conclude they are displaying what they call "statistical discrimination" (i.e., the police are operating on the basis of class probability) rather than racial prejudice. Perhaps more to the point, they conclude that the police are primarily motivated by a desire to maximize drug arrests.

Some racial profiling defenders agree that the drug war bears a large part of the blame for racial profiling. "Many of the stop-and-search cases that brought this matter into the headlines were part of the so-called war on drugs," writes Derbyshire. "The police procedures behind them were ratified by court decisions of the 1980s, themselves mostly responding to the rising tide of illegal narcotics." But Derbyshire dismisses the argument that racial profiling is *chiefly* a byproduct of the drug war. He contends that even if drugs were legalized tomorrow, the practice would continue.

He is confusing the two forms of police procedure we have outlined above. The practice of laying out broad dragnets to see what turns up would almost entirely disappear but for the attempt to stamp out drug trafficking and use. Derbyshire, to bolster his case, cites the fact that in 1997, "Blacks, who are 13 percent of the U.S. population, comprised 35 percent of those arrested for embezzlement." This statistic would be useful if he were defending the fact that 35 percent of those investigated for embezzling that year were black. But does Derbyshire believe that stopping random blacks on an interstate highway is catching very many embezzlers? Or that, absent the drug war, cops would start searching cars they pull over for embezzled funds?

How asset forfeiture fuels profiling

In the 1980s, state legislatures and congress were frustrated with their inability to arrest and convict "drug kingpins," so they passed laws that gave police the power to seize the property of suspected dealers. The dubious rationale: the "pushers'" property had been purchased through ill-gotten gains and hence didn't rightly belong to them. (questions about establishing actual guilt were brushed aside as counterproductive.) the federal comprehensive crime act of 1984 was the most important of these measures, as it allowed local police agencies that cooperated in a drug investigation to keep the vast majority of the assets seized.

In addition, the Department of Justice decided that police in states that did not allow their agencies to keep asset forfeiture proceeds could have the feds "adopt" their seizures. The *Kansas City Star*'s Karen Dillon has done extensive investigative reporting on asset forfeiture. . . . She writes: "Wisconsin law mandates that forfeiture money goes to public schools, but only $16,906 went into Wisconsin's education fund during the year ending in June 1999, according to the state treasury department. During just six months of the same period, local law enforcement gave the federal government $1.5 million in seizures."

> *One document, used for training, teaches [New Jersey state] troopers to zero in on minorities when scanning state roadways for possible drug traffickers.*

In a paper published in the September 2000 issue of the economics journal *Public Choice*, "Entrepreneurial Police and Drug Enforcement Policy," Brent D. Mast, Bruce L. Benson, and David W. Rasmussen report that forfeiture receipts roughly doubled every year for several years after the passage of the Comprehensive Crime Act. According to the *Sourcebook of Criminal Justice Statistics*, the total value of Drug Enforcement Administration seizures reached nearly $1 billion in 1992. A large amount of that revenue flows back from the federal government to state and local police departments. Dillon notes: "In 1997 and 1998, the St. Louis Metropolitan Police Department received back more than $2.5 million. In 1998 alone, the Georgia Bureau of Investigation took back $1.7 million."

A letter to the International Narcotics Interdiction Association (INIA) from the Richmond Metro Interdiction Unit, posted on INIA's Web site, is accompanied by a photo of two cops in front of a pile of $298,440. The letter says: "We took this money off a guy coming from NY to Miami on Amtrak about two weeks after returning from SKY NARC [an INIA training session] in Anaheim. It was a great school and as you can see it paid off."

The U.S. Department of Justice reports: "Collectively, local police departments received $490 million worth of cash, goods, and property from drug asset forfeiture programs during fiscal 1997. Sheriffs' departments had total receipts of $158 million."

This kind of money adds a major incentive to police efforts to discover drug crimes. The study by Mast, Benson, and Rasmussen concludes: "The results for the impact of asset seizure laws are robust. . . . Police focus relatively more effort on drug control when they can enhance their budgets by retaining seized assets. Legislation permitting police to keep a portion of seized assets raises drug arrests as a portion of total arrests by about 20 percent and drug arrest rates by about 18 percent."

Of course, if the police begin harassing all motorists in a particular locale, support for their activities will soon evaporate. However, if they can identify a minority group that is somewhat more likely to commit a particular drug crime—and if they know that members of that group are not politically powerful—then the police can focus on those people in order to enhance their departmental revenue.

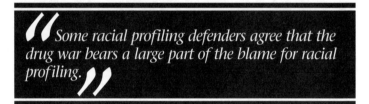

Some racial profiling defenders agree that the drug war bears a large part of the blame for racial profiling.

The usual supposition, that the accused is innocent until proven guilty, has been explicitly reversed in asset forfeiture cases. The authorities are not required to prove that a crime, involving the goods in question, has been committed. Instead, they must merely have "probable cause" for the seizure; the burden of proof is on the defendant trying to recover his property. The Schaffer Library of Drug Policy (druglibrary.org/schaffer) has found that 80 percent of those who have had assets seized are never charged with a crime, let alone convicted of one. Federal law provides for up to five years in prison for attempting to prevent one's own property from being grabbed.

It did not take long for those in law enforcement to conclude that their best haul would come from seizing goods from citizens who lack the resources to win them back. In one highly publicized case that occurred in 1991, federal authorities at the Nashville airport took more than $9,000 in cash from Willie Jones, a black landscaper who was flying to Houston in order to purchase shrubs. According to the police, that money *could* have been used to purchase drugs. After spending thousands of dollars and two years on the case, the landscaper was able to convince the courts to return *most* of the seized cash.

Sam Thach, a Vietnamese immigrant, found himself in a

similar situation [in 2000]. He was relieved of $147,000 by the DEA while traveling on Amtrak. Thach was investigated because the details of his ticket purchase, which Amtrak shared with the DEA, "fit the profile" of a drug courier. He was not charged with any crime and is now fighting to retrieve his money in federal court.

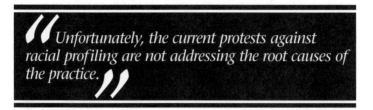

Unfortunately, the current protests against racial profiling are not addressing the root causes of the practice.

When the University of Pennsylvania study and the study by Mast, Benson, and Rasmussen are considered in tandem, the implication is clear. The possibility of rich pickings through asset forfeiture, combined with the higher propensity for black motorists to carry drugs, provides police departments with a tremendous incentive to engage in racial profiling. It is hardly surprising, then, that police take the bait, even at the cost of racial bias accusations and investigations.

[In 2000], in reaction to high-profile cases of abuse, Congress passed legislation that changed the standard in federal civil asset forfeiture cases. Rather than showing "probable cause" that property was connected to a crime, the feds must now demonstrate "by a preponderance of the evidence" that the property was used in or is the product of a crime, a significantly higher legal standard. The revised law also awards legal fees to defendants who successfully challenge property seizures and gives judges more latitude to return seized property. Exactly what effect the law will have on federal agents, or on state and local cops, is not yet clear.

This is your law enforcement on drugs

In the panic created by the drug war, our traditional liberties have been eroded. Rather than regarding case probability as a necessary component of probable cause for searches or seizures, the American law enforcement system has now come to accept class probability as sufficient justification for many intrusions.

Unfortunately, the current protests against racial profiling are not addressing the root causes of the practice. Politicians, eager to please voters, have created potentially greater problems by trying to suppress the symptoms. As John Derbyshire points out, the laws rushed onto the books to end racial profiling result in severe obstacles to police officers attempting to investigate serious crimes. He notes, "In Philadelphia, a federal court order now requires police to fill out both sides of an 8-½-by-11 sheet on every citizen contact." Unless our solution to this problem addresses its cause, we will be faced with the choice of either hindering important police work or treating some of our citizens, based on characteristics (race, age, and so on) completely beyond their control, in a manner that is patently unfair.

If we really wish to end the scourge of racial profiling, we must address its roots: drug laws that encourage police to consider members of broad groups as probable criminals. We must redirect law enforcement toward solving specific, known crimes using the particular evidence available to them about that crime. Whatever one's opinion on drug legalization may be, it's easy to agree that the state of seizure law in America is reprehensible, even given [2000's] federal reforms. It should be obvious that there's something nutty about a legal system that assumes suspects in murder, robbery, and rape cases are innocent until a trial proves otherwise, but assumes that a landscaper carrying some cash is guilty of drug trafficking.

Drugs, prohibitionists commonly point out, can damage a user's mind. They apparently can have the same effect on the minds of law enforcement officials.

7

Racial Profiling Is Not Racist

John Derbyshire

John Derbyshire is a novelist and a contributing editor to the National Review, *a conservative weekly magazine.*

Critics decry racial profiling by police as a discriminatory practice that especially targets young African Americans. However, statistics prove that young black men commit a disproportionate number of crimes. Therefore, racial profiling is a legitimate policing tool. The recent outcry against racial profiling is simply the latest example of liberal oversensitivity to racial issues.

"Racial profiling" has become one of the shibboleths of our time. Anyone who wants a public career in the United States must place himself on record as being against it. Thus, ex-senator John Ashcroft, on the eve of his confirmation hearings [for Attorney General]: "It's wrong, inappropriate, shouldn't be done." During the vice-presidential debate [in October 2000,] moderator Bernard Shaw invited the candidates to imagine themselves black victims of racial profiling. Both made the required ritual protestations of outrage. [Joe] Lieberman: "I have a few African-American friends who have gone through this horror, and you know, it makes me want to kind of hit the wall, because it is such an assault on their humanity and their citizenship." [Dick] Cheney: "It's the sense of anger and frustration and rage that would go with knowing that the only reason you were stopped . . . was because of the color of your skin. . . ." In the strange, rather depressing, pattern these things al-

John Derbyshire, "In Defense of Racial Profiling: Where Is Our Common Sense?" *National Review*, February 19, 2001. Copyright © 2001 by National Review, Inc., 215 Lexington Avenue, New York, NY 10016. Reproduced by permission.

ways follow nowadays, the American public has speedily swung into line behind the Pied Pipers: Gallup reports that 81 percent of the public disapproves of racial profiling.

The history of the term

All of which represents an extraordinary level of awareness of, and hostility to, and even passion against ("hit the wall . . .") a practice that, up to about [the mid-1990s,] practically nobody had heard of. It is, in fact, instructive to begin by looking at the history of this shibboleth. . . .

The career of the term "racial profiling" seems to have begun in 1994, but did not really take off until April 1998, when two white New Jersey state troopers pulled over a van for speeding. As they approached the van from behind, it suddenly reversed towards them. The troopers fired eleven shots from their handguns, wounding three of the van's four occupants, who were all black or Hispanic. The troopers, James Kenna and John Hogan, subsequently became poster boys for the "racial profiling" lobbies, facing the same indignities, though so far with less serious consequences, as were endured by the Los Angeles policemen in the Rodney King case: endless investigations, double jeopardy, and so on.

Practically all law-enforcement professionals believe in the need for racial profiling.

And a shibboleth was born. News-media databases list only a scattering of instances of the term "racial profiling" from 1994 to 1998. In that latter year, the number hit double digits, and thereafter rose quickly into the hundreds and thousands. Now we all know about it, and we are, of course, all against it.

Not everyone opposes profiling

Well, not quite all. American courts—including (see below) the U.S. Supreme Court—are not against it. Jurisprudence on the matter is pretty clear: So long as race is only one factor in a generalized approach to the questioning of suspects, it may be considered. And of course, pace Candidate Cheney, it always is only one factor. I have been unable to locate any statistics on the point, but I feel sure that elderly black women are stopped by the police much less often than are young white men.

Even in the political sphere, where truth-telling and independent thinking on matters of race have long been liabilities, there are those who refuse to mouth the required pieties. Alan Keyes, when asked by Larry King if he would be angry with a police officer who pulled him over for being black, replied: "I was raised that everything I did represented my family, my race, and my country. I would be angry with the people giving me a bad reputation."

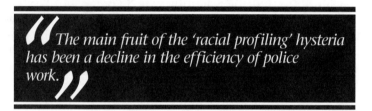

The main fruit of the 'racial profiling' hysteria has been a decline in the efficiency of police work.

Practically all law-enforcement professionals believe in the need for racial profiling. In an article on the topic for the *New York Times Magazine* in June 1999, Jeffrey Goldberg interviewed Bernard Parks, chief of the Los Angeles Police Department. Parks, who is black, asked rhetorically of racial profiling: "Should we play the percentages? . . . It's common sense." Note that date, though. This was pretty much the latest time at which it was possible for a public official to speak truthfully about racial profiling. Law-enforcement professionals were learning the importance of keeping their thoughts to themselves. Four months before the Goldberg piece saw print, New Jersey state-police superintendent Carl Williams, in an interview, said that certain crimes were associated with certain ethnic groups, and that it was naive to think that race was not an issue in policing—both statements, of course, perfectly true. Supt. Williams was fired the same day by Gov. Christie Todd Whitman.

Stereotypes are useful tools

Like other race issues in the U.S., racial profiling is a "tadpole," with an enormous black head and a long but comparatively inconsequential brown, yellow, and red tail. While Hispanic, "Asian-American," and other lesser groups have taken up the "racial profiling" chant with gusto, the crux of the matter is the resentment that black Americans feel toward the attentions of white policemen. By far the largest number of Americans angry about racial profiling are law-abiding black people who feel that they are stopped and questioned because the police regard all black people with undue suspicion. They feel that they are the victims of a negative stereotype.

They are. Unfortunately, a negative stereotype can be correct, and even useful. I was surprised to find, when researching this [viewpoint,] that within the academic field of social psychology there is a large literature on stereotypes, and that much of it—an entire school of thought—holds that stereotypes are essential life tools. On the scientific evidence, the primary function of stereotypes is what researchers call "the reality function." That is, stereotypes are useful tools for dealing with the world. Confronted with a snake or a fawn, our immediate behavior is determined by generalized beliefs—stereotypes—about snakes and fawns. Stereotypes are, in fact, merely one aspect of the mind's ability to make generalizations, without which science and mathematics, not to mention, as the snake/fawn example shows, much of everyday life, would be impossible.

At some level, everybody knows this stuff, even the guardians of the "racial profiling" flame. Jesse Jackson famously, in 1993, confessed that: "There is nothing more painful to me at this stage in my life than to walk down the street and hear footsteps and start thinking about robbery, then look around and see somebody white and feel relieved." Here is Sandra Seegars of the Washington, D.C., Taxicab Commission:

"Late at night, if I saw young black men dressed in a slovenly way, I wouldn't pick them up. . . . And during the day, I'd think twice about it."

Pressed to define "slovenly," Ms. Seegars elaborated thus: "A young black guy with his hat on backwards, shirttail hanging down longer than his coat, baggy pants down below his underwear, and unlaced tennis shoes." Now there's a stereotype for you! Ms. Seegars is, of course, black.

An efficient tactic

Law-enforcement officials are simply employing the same stereotypes as you, me, Jesse, and Sandra, but taking the opposite course of action. What we seek to avoid, they pursue. They do this for reasons of simple efficiency. A policeman who concentrates a disproportionate amount of his limited time and resources on young black men is going to uncover far more crimes—and therefore be far more successful in his career—than one who biases his attention toward, say, middle-aged Asian women. It is, as Chief Parks said, common sense.

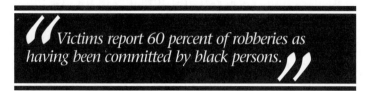

Victims report 60 percent of robberies as having been committed by black persons.

Similarly with the tail of the tadpole-racial-profiling issues that do not involve black people. China is known to have obtained a top-secret warhead design. Among those with clearance to work on that design are people from various kinds of national and racial background. Which ones should investigators concentrate on? The Swedes? The answer surely is: They should first check out anyone who has family or friends in China, who has made trips to China, or who has met with Chinese officials. This would include me, for example—my father-in-law is an official of the Chinese Communist Party. Would I then have been "racially profiled"?

Statistics lead to uncertainty

It is not very surprising to learn that the main fruit of the "racial profiling" hysteria has been a decline in the efficiency of police work. In Philadelphia, a federal court order now requires police to fill out both sides of an 8½-by-11 sheet on every citizen contact. Law-enforcement agencies nationwide are engaged in similar statistics-gathering exercises, under pressure from federal lawmakers like U.S. Rep. John Conyers, who has announced that he will introduce a bill to force police agencies to keep detailed information about traffic stops. ("The struggle goes on," declared Rep. Conyers. The struggle that is going on, it sometimes seems, is a struggle to prevent our police forces from accomplishing any useful work at all.)

The mountain of statistics that is being brought forth by all this panic does not, on the evidence so far, seem likely to shed much light on what is happening. The numbers have a way of leading off into infinite regresses of uncertainty. The city of San Jose, Calif., for example, discovered that, yes, the percentage of blacks being stopped was higher than their representation in the city's population. Ah, but patrol cars were computer-assigned to high-crime districts, which are mainly inhabited by minorities. So that over-representation might actually be an under-representation! But then, minorities have fewer cars. . . .

Notwithstanding the extreme difficulty of finding out what is actually happening, we can at least seek some moral and philosophical grounds on which to take a stand either for or against racial profiling. I am going to take it as a given that most readers of this article will be of a conservative inclination, and shall offer only those arguments likely to appeal to persons so inclined. If you seek arguments of other kinds, they are not hard to find—just pick up your newspaper or turn on your TV.

Not a by-product of drug war

Of arguments against racial profiling, probably the ones most persuasive to a conservative are the ones from libertarianism. Many of the stop-and-search cases that brought this matter into the headlines were part of the so-called war on drugs. The police procedures behind them were ratified by court decisions of the 1980s, themselves mostly responding to the rising tide of illegal narcotics. In *U.S. vs. Montoya De Hernandez* (1985) for example, Chief Justice [William] Rehnquist validated the detention of a suspected "balloon swallowing" drug courier until the material had passed through her system, by noting previous invasions upheld by the Court:

> [F]irst class mail may be opened without a warrant on less than probable cause. . . . Automotive travellers may be stopped . . . near the border without individualized suspicion *even if the stop is based largely on ethnicity*. . . . (My italics.)

The Chief Justice further noted that these incursions are in response to "the veritable national crisis in law enforcement caused by smuggling of illegal narcotics." Many on the political Right feel that the war on drugs is at best misguided, at worst a moral and constitutional disaster. Yet it is naive to imagine that the "racial profiling" hubbub would go away, or even much diminish, if all state and federal drug laws were repealed tomorrow. Black and Hispanic Americans would still be committing crimes at rates higher than citizens of other races. The differential criminality of various ethnic groups is not only, or even mainly located in drug crimes. In 1997, for example, blacks, who are 13 percent of the U.S. population, comprised 35 percent of those arrested for embezzlement. (It is not generally appreciated that black Americans commit higher levels not only of "street crime," but also of white-collar crime.)

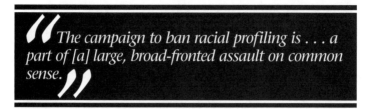

The campaign to ban racial profiling is . . . a part of [a] large, broad-fronted assault on common sense.

Even without the drug war, diligent police officers would still, therefore, be correct to regard black and Hispanic citizens—other factors duly considered—as more likely to be breaking the law. The Chinese government would still be trying to recruit spies exclusively from among Chinese-born Americans. (The Chinese Communist Party is, in this respect, the keenest "racial profiler" of all.) . . .

Outlaw the practice?

The best non-libertarian argument against racial profiling is the one from equality before the law. This has been most cogently presented by Prof. Randall Kennedy of Harvard. Kennedy concedes most of the points I have made. Yes, he says:

> Statistics abundantly confirm that African Americans—and particularly young black men—commit a dramatically disproportionate share of street crime in the United States. This is a sociological fact, not a figment of the media's (or the police's) racist imagination. In recent years, for example, victims of crime report blacks as the perpetrators in around 25 percent of the violent crimes suffered, although blacks constitute only about twelve percent of the nation's population.

And yes, says Prof. Kennedy, outlawing racial profiling will reduce the efficiency of police work. Nonetheless, for constitutional and moral reasons we should outlaw the practice. If this places extra burdens on law enforcement, well, "racial equality, like all good things in life, costs something; it does not come for free."

There are two problems with this. The first is that Kennedy has minimized the black-white difference in criminality, and therefore that "cost." I don't know where his 25 percent comes from, or what "recent years" means, but I do know that in Department of Justice figures for 1997, victims report 60 percent of robberies as having been committed by black persons. In that same year, a black American was eight times more likely than a non-black to commit homicide—and "non-black" here includes Hispanics, not broken out separately in these figures. A racial-profiling ban, under which police officers were required to stop and question suspects in precise proportion to their demographic representation (in what? the precinct population? the state population? the national population?), would lead to massive inefficiencies in police work. Which is to say, massive declines in the apprehension of criminals.

Race is not a special status

The other problem is with the special status that Prof. Kennedy accords to race. Kennedy: "Racial distinctions are and should be different from other lines of social stratification." Thus, if it can be shown, as it surely can, that state troopers stop young people more than old people, relative to young people's numerical representation on the road being patrolled, that is of no consequence. If they stop black people more than white people, on the same criterion, that is of large consequence. This, in spite of the fact that the categories "age" and "race" are both rather fuzzy (define "young") and are both useful predictors of criminality. In spite of the fact, too, that the principle of equality before the law does not, and up to now has never been thought to, guarantee equal outcomes for any law-enforcement process, only that a citizen who has come under reasonable suspicion will be treated fairly.

It is on this special status accorded to race that, I believe, we have gone most seriously astray. I am willing, in fact, to say much more than this: In the matter of race, I think the Anglo-Saxon world has taken leave of its senses. The campaign to ban racial profiling is, as I see it, a part of that large, broad-fronted assault on common sense that our over-educated over-lawyered society has been enduring for some forty years now, and whose roots are in a fanatical egalitarianism, a grim determination not to face up to the realities of group differences, a theological attachment to the doctrine that the sole and sufficient explanation for all such differences is "racism"—which is to say, the malice and cruelty of white people—and a nursed and petted guilt towards the behavior of our ancestors.

At present, Americans are drifting away from the concept of belonging to a single nation. I do not think this drift will be arrested until we can shed the idea that deference to the sensitivities of racial minorities—however overwrought those sensitivities may be, however over-stimulated by unscrupulous mountebanks, however disconnected from reality—trumps every other consideration, including even the maintenance of social order. To shed that idea, we must confront our national hysteria about race, which causes large numbers of otherwise sane people to believe that the hearts of their fellow citizens are filled with malice towards them. So long as we continue to pander to that poisonous, preposterous belief, we shall only wander off deeper into a wilderness of division, mistrust, and institutionalized rancor—that wilderness, the most freshly painted signpost to which bears the legend RACIAL PROFILING.

The Rise of White Nationalist Groups Is a Significant Problem

Carol M. Swain

Carol M. Swain is a professor of political science and a professor of law at Vanderbilt University. Swain is the author of Black Faces, Black Interests: The Representation of African Americans in Congress *and the editor of* Race Versus Class: The New Affirmative Action Debate.

The emerging white nationalist movement in America poses a serious threat to race relations. Perverting the language of multiculturalism and civil rights activism, this movement has the potential to attract mainstream white Americans, who are increasingly frustrated by difficult economic times, an influx of illegal immigrants, and urban violence. In many ways, the white supremacist movement has simply been repackaged, but the radicalism of their views remains much the same.

The conference brought some of the leading intellectual and political lights of the white far right. . . . They talked about an America that they believe once was and ever ought to be a white, European-American nation. Theirs would be a nation bound by blood and sanctified by genetic scientists who appeared before them as a place where white people might rightly prevail over the black and brown people; a nation where what they consider the nat-

Carol M. Swain, *The New White Nationalism in America: Its Challenge to Integration.* Cambridge, UK: Cambridge University Press, 2002. Copyright © 2002 by Carol M. Swain. Reproduced by permission of the publisher.

ural hierarchy might finally triumph over what they
count as the false promise of egalitarianism.
— Jonathan Tilove, American Renaissance
Conference, spring 2000

Over the past ten years a new white racial advocacy movement has gained strength in the United States that poses a
severe challenge to the ideals of an integrated society. Many of
the leaders of this new movement, which is called "white nationalism" here, are very different from the sorts of people we
have come to associate with the traditional racist right in America. Cultured, intelligent, and often possessing impressive degrees from some of America's premier colleges and universities,
this new breed of white racial advocate is a far cry from the pop-
ulist politicians and hooded Klansmen of the Old South who
fought the losing battles for segregation and white supremacy
during the great civil rights upheavals of a generation ago. The
new white nationalists differ even more from the small band of
misfits and psychopaths who formed the heart of the ineffec-
tual neo-Nazi movement of that era. While sharing much in
common with the older style of white racist and white supremacy movement, and drawing upon important white supremacist
beliefs, the new white nationalism is potentially broader in its
appeal and a development sufficiently different from the older
racist right to be considered a distinct phenomenon. The new
white nationalism, in this sense, might be considered a kind of
repackaged, relabeled, and transformed white supremacy that is
aiming its appeal at a broader and better-educated audience. . . .

I argue here that however educated and nonviolent they
may be, we should be as concerned about the new white nationalists and their organizations as we are about individuals in
traditional white supremacy and hate groups. The polish and
sophistication of some of the new white nationalism, their separatist agenda, and their ability to disguise themselves and
move freely within many mainstream institutions poses a major threat to racial harmony, I believe, in our increasingly multiethnic, multiracial society.

Characteristics of the new white nationalism

With some important exceptions, these new racial activists call
themselves "white nationalists" or "white racialists" rather than
"white supremacists" because they believe that the concept of

"racial nationalism" captures their core beliefs in racial self-determination and self-preservation better than any supremacist or segregationist label. Contemporary white nationalists draw upon the potent rhetoric of national self-determination and national self-assertion in an attempt to protect what they believe is their God-given natural right to their distinct cultural, political, and genetic identity as white Europeans. This identity, they believe, is gravely threatened in contemporary America by the rise of multiculturalism, affirmative action policies that favor minorities, large-scale immigration into the United States from non-white nations, racial intermarriage, and the identity politics pursued by rival racial and ethnic groups.

> *A new white racial advocacy movement . . . poses a severe challenge to the ideals of an integrated society.*

Above all, white nationalists are driven by a sense of urgency. America, they believe, is fast becoming a nation dominated by nonwhite people. Since they believe that it is the white blood and white genes—and the white culture these have created—that are responsible for America's past greatness and success as a nation, this development can have only catastrophic consequences, according to their reckoning. The black and brown peoples of the world, they contend, are morally and intellectually inferior to whites and Asians, and thus the more numerous and influential they become, the more American society will degenerate. The fact that demographic trends project European Americans gradually becoming a minority over the next several decades is viewed with horror. "Our children . . . will live in an America where alien cultures will not simply be present, but will dominate us," warns former Klansman David Duke, who now describes himself as a white nationalist. "This alien influx," he goes on, "is a disaster for our country, our people, our families."

A similar observation is offered by Jared Taylor, the founder and editor of *American Renaissance* magazine, the most important organ of the new white nationalism. Powerful forces are destroying both "European man and European civilization" on the American continent, Taylor declares. "If we do nothing the nation we leave our grandchildren will be a grim

Third World failure, in which whites will be the minority . . . [and Western Civilization, if it exists at all,] will be a faint echo."

Within the white nationalist movement are fresh-faced converts from academia including Professors Michael H. Hart, Michael Levin, J. Philippe Rushton, and Glayde Whitney, who share many of the beliefs of traditional white supremacists, especially their negative assessments of African Americans. These scholars believe the main reason black people today are plagued by such high incidence of criminal violence, out-of-wedlock births, poor school performance, and AIDS is rooted in their differential genetic endowment. The process of human evolution, as it has adapted to different ecological circumstances, has produced, they contend, a distinct racial hierarchy in terms of innate intelligence, the ability to delay gratification, to control emotions, and to plan for the future, with North Asians at the top of the hierarchy, white Europeans somewhere below them, Hispanics significantly below the white Europeans, and black Africans and their recent descendants at the very bottom.

> *[White nationalists claim] the black and brown peoples of the world, they contend, are morally and intellectually inferior to whites and Asians.*

Besides their belief in the biogenetically determined inequality of the races, white nationalists believe that race is a legitimate criteria for inclusion within the civil community and that nations are least faction-ridden when a given territory is dominated by a single race or ethnic group. A country that embarks on a policy of encouraging racial and ethnic diversity within its borders through liberal immigration policies is courting national disaster, they contend. To cite Jared Taylor again:

Up until 1965, we had an immigration policy that was designed . . . to keep the country white. I see absolutely nothing wrong with that. In fact, I think that's a healthy, normal and natural position for a country to take. I think Japan should stay Japanese. I think Mexico should stay Mexican. Some think somehow that it's virtuous of the United States, after having been founded and built by Europeans, according to European institutions, to reinvent itself or transform itself into a non-white country with a Third World population. I think that's a kind of cultural and racial national suicide. . . . Wherever you go, wherever you mix racial groups, you're going to have tensions, you're going to have friction, and to have an immigration policy that imports millions of people of all sorts of different racial and ethnic groups, I think, it's bound to cause racial tension. . . . We're all now more or less obliged to say, "Oh! Diversity is a wonderful thing for the country," whereas, practically every example of tension, bloodshed, civil unrest around the world is due to precisely the kind of thing we're importing—diversity.

White nationalists recognize that America is already a multiracial, multiethnic society, but given their pessimism about the long-term health and viability of such societies, they believe that drastic measures must be taken to change things. Their solution is usually some form of ethnic separatism based on territorial partition. Racial separation is the obvious next step for people who believe that racial and ethnic minorities are a danger to the personal safety and social values of white Americans. The logic of the separatists' argument is well captured by American Enterprise Institute scholar Dinesh D'Souza in summing up the ideology that pervades *American Renaissance:* "Western civilization is inherently white, America was founded on white norms, immigrants are perennial outsiders, blacks are 'Africans in America,' they are in America but not of America, race determines culture, miscegenation and intermarriage are an abomination, and racial separatism, preferably separate black and white nations, is the answer."

White nationalists will often invoke the statesmen of America's founding generation to support their contention that a multiracial America, one involving the successful integration of blacks and whites, is not a viable option. Indeed, many of the new white nationalists see themselves as true patriots who seek to preserve the kind of European-dominated society that the founding generation bequeathed to posterity but which is now threatened with destruction. They seek to preserve an America—or a segment of America—where white, European Americans would be able to develop freely their common culture and common political life without hindrance from members of other racial groups, particularly the black and brown groups. This, they say, is the kind of America that statesmen like Washington and Jefferson originally envisioned, though their true views, they charge, have long been forgotten or suppressed by those who would force America into a multiculturalist mode.

Difference between white supremists and white nationalists

Don Black, the founder of the Stormfront website, expresses this view very clearly. Black, a former Klansman who, like David Duke, now calls himself a white nationalist, was asked by our interviewer whether or not he accepted the term "white supremacist" as an accurate description of his views. He responded that he was a racial nationalist, not a white supremacist, and that all he and other white nationalists were demanding was the preservation of the kind of white America envisioned by many of the great statesmen of America's past. . . .

Racial partitioning

One of the most influential arguments for the racial partitioning of the United States has been made by Michael H. Hart, a retired professor of astrophysics, who holds advanced degrees in physics, computer science, and law. Hart has argued that a "multiracial state hurts all of us, and it hurts whites in particular." Whites, he says, have to put up with much higher crime rates because of the presence in America of large numbers of nonwhites. They have to put up with higher incidence of many social problems, including illegitimacy, welfare dependency, and declining standards in schools. All this could be avoided, Hart claims, by the racial partitioning of America. He has proposed partitioning America into four parts that would provide for a black-dominated state, a white-dominated state, an Hispanic-dominated state, and an integrated, mixed-race state for all those who genuinely prefer a multicultural arrangement.

Hart distinguishes between a nation, in the sense of an ethnically self-consciousness group of individuals who consider themselves to be a distinct people, and a state, in the sense of a centralized government ruling over a territory. "The Norwegians," he writes, "are a nation, and they have their own state,

Norway. The Kurds are a nation, but they do not have their own independent state. Rwanda, in Africa, is a state containing two national groups, the Hutu and the Tutsi. India, Nigeria, the former Soviet Union, and the former Yugoslavia are, or were, multinational states." The history of states that contain within their borders more than one nation, Hart believes, is not an encouraging one. "Most binational and multinational states do not work well, but are beset by endless ethnic strife, often quite bloody."

African Americans already behave as if they constitute a separate nation, Hart contends, and it is for this reason that separation is called for. As evidence for a distinct black nation-consciousness Hart cites the African-American middle class's embrace of the black holiday of Kwanza, the existence of a black flag and a black national anthem, demands for Afrocentric curriculums, and demands for quotas in hiring, promotions, and college admissions. When combined with the considerable degree of support that black communities have shown over the years for black nationalist figures such as Marcus Garvey, Elijah Muhammad, and Louis Farrakhan, the case, he believes, is clinched: Blacks constitute a separate and alien nation that cannot be integrated into white America.

> *We should be as concerned about the new white nationalists . . . as we are about . . . traditional white supremacy and hate groups.*

Like other white nationalists, Hart is particularly insistent on describing himself as a separatist rather than a supremacist. "I, like most other white separatists," he told our interviewer, "resent being called a white *supremacist*. . . . I have no desire to rule over blacks, or to attempt to rule over blacks, or have someone else rule over blacks in my behalf. Quite the contrary, I want to have complete independence. All that I—and most white separatists—want is the opportunity to rule ourselves, in our own independent country. Far from wishing to extend our rule, we are quite willing to give up much of the territory that American whites already control. All we want is to live in peace in our own country, and to trade with foreign countries on mutually acceptable terms. . . . I do not want to rule, enslave, or exterminate anyone."

Hart's views are similar to those of other white nationalists, as well as to those of white racists and white supremacists of the older style, many of whom have advocated partitioning the United States into separate nations. The Pacific Northwest is the section of the country that they usually single out as the territory for an all-white nation because of its current low concentration of nonwhites.

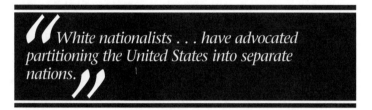

White nationalists . . . have advocated partitioning the United States into separate nations.

A belief that racial integration has not and cannot work in the United States and that racial separatism is the only answer joins many contemporary white nationalists with black nationalists, past and present. "White racism and black racism are now mirror ideologies," Dinesh D'Souza writes. This development, however, is nothing new, as black nationalists and white racists have always shared much in common. Since the days of Marcus Garvey and his back-to-Africa movement in the 1920s, Klansmen and members of other white racist groups have periodically gotten together with members of black nationalist groups to affirm their common goal of preserving racial purity. . . .

Expanding the appeal of white nationalism

In his 1995 book somewhat misleadingly titled *The End of Racism*, Dinesh D'Souza concludes that "white racism is not dead, but, as many blacks suspect, it now wears a different face." This is an accurate description of much of the new white nationalism and white racial advocacy. Since the 1980s, much has changed in the world of the racist right. Many former white supremacists such as Don Black and David Duke have changed with the times and reinvented themselves as white nationalists or white civil rights crusaders. With the change to nationalism and civil rights advocacy has come the adoption of new tactics, new symbols, and new language designed to allay the fears of citizens repelled by more extremist approaches characteristic of the older racist right. While the older style of racist right certainly lives on and has its audience, for many middle-class and better-educated Americans it has little appeal.

Much of the new white nationalism, by contrast, is a more sophisticated enterprise that has much greater possibility of winning over large numbers of middle-class, white Americans. Unlike the older racist right epitomized by the 1950s- and 1960s-era Ku Klux Klan, the new white nationalist movement that has emerged in America over the past two decades is preeminently a movement of discourse and ideas. It seeks to expand its audience largely through argument and persuasion directed at its target audience of white Americans who have become angered over race-based affirmative action policy and impending demographic change. In this regard, it is more akin to Leftist and Green parties around the world than to the older style of white supremacy groups. The new white nationalists are skillfully using the rhetoric of civil rights, national self-determination, and ethnic identity politics as they make their case among the many aggrieved whites in America for a white, European-centered nation.

> *Wary of the ignorant, redneck image, white nationalists and white power advocates today are seeking a more educated class of converts.*

It is important to grasp what a radical makeover this represents, at least in style, from the older racist right movement. The older racist and anti-Semitic right, represented by organizations like the Klan and Nazi Party, made its appeal primarily through fiery speeches and emotional rhetoric with minimal rational content. A few well-chosen slogans endlessly repeated and prominently displayed formed the ideological backbone of the movement: "Niggers in Their Place," "White Men Built This Country," "Jews Get Out!," "Segregation Now, Segregation Tomorrow, Segregation Forever." In addition, secret initiations and rituals, flamboyant costumes, and mass parades formed important aspects of the movement's activities that for many members, at least, offered the additional allurement of an intimate fraternal order or esoteric club. There was very little in the way of intellectual content, and not surprisingly, the audience remained largely lower-class and uneducated. Many of the newer white nationalist groups, by contrast, seek a broader and more influential audience, and as Americans have become more educated, their approach has adjusted accordingly.

Unlike the older racist right, the Americans that many white nationalists would most like to recruit as activists are not those at the margins of society. Apparently wary of the ignorant, redneck image, white nationalists and white power advocates today are seeking a more educated class of converts and spokespersons in order to attract a potentially more influential following among the young. Although Joe Six-pack is still welcomed into the ranks of most white nationalist and white racist organizations, he is not being encouraged to appear on talk shows and present himself as the standard bearer of white racial advocacy. Today's white nationalist recruit could just as easily be a graduate of an Ivy League college who wears an expensive suit and sports a Rolex as a high school dropout who works a gas pump at the local filling station. As Mark Potok of the Southern Poverty Law Center has remarked, many of the new recruits to some of the newer white racist and white supremacy groups "are not people who live in trailers. There is a concerted effort . . . to recruit college-bound middle- and upper-middle-class kids."

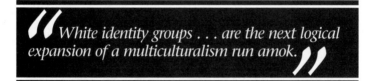

White identity groups . . . are the next logical expansion of a multiculturalism run amok.

The rise in the caliber of recruits parallels the rise in the caliber of the new white nationalist leadership. Not only are many leaders of the new white nationalist and white supremacy groups better educated than their predecessors of a generation ago, but they are often more personable and more appealing as human beings as well. This last point may be difficult to grasp since it has been distorted in many ways by some of the watchdog groups that help keep us informed of what those on the racist right are up to. As Jeffrey Kaplan and Leonard Weinberg explain in *The Emergence of a Euro-American Radical Right*, our image of what is going on among members of the contemporary racist and racial-nationalist right may be influenced heavily by watchdog agencies such as the Simon Wiesenthal Center, SOS Racism, Klanwatch, and the Anti-Defamation League of B'nai Brith. These organizations, Kaplan and Weinberg explain, are intensely hostile to the people and organizations they monitor and they have a tendency to portray them in the worst possible light. The goal of these watchdog agencies, they say, "is to have members of the public regard the racist and anti-Semitic right with the same affection they would the AIDS epidemic or the outbreak of the ebola fever." Kaplan and Weinberg, however, point out the shortcomings of this strategy: "There is a price to be paid for reducing the groups and individuals involved to screen villains straight out of Central Casting. The price is that these efforts distort the reality." The reality, Kaplan and Weinberg explain, is that many of the individuals and groups that make up the contemporary racist right "are often more complicated, considerably more personable, and far more nuanced" than is suggested by the negative stereotypes.

> *Potential converts to white nationalism can be found among the millions of frustrated white Americans who have supported mainstream conservative political candidates.*

Sociologists Betty Dobratz and Stephanie Shanks-Meile, who conducted participant observations and many interviews with white supremacists, had an assessment similar to that of Kaplan and Weinberg. They found that their subjects deviated considerably from the caricaturist stereotypes of the watchdog agencies and were considerably more personable than expected.

Any attempt to weigh the seriousness of the threat posed by the new white nationalism must take into account how certain groups are transforming themselves in order to widen their appeal. If observers limit themselves to monitoring the more extremist groups or those espousing more virulent forms of racial hatred, the seriousness of the problem currently confronting America will be greatly underestimated. To increase their appeal, some white nationalist groups are disguising themselves and adopting names less racially inflammatory than "Ku Klux Klan" or "Aryan Nations." A growing number of white nationalist and white supremacy groups have adopted innocuous-sounding names such as the Euro-American Student Union, the Institute for Historical Review (a Holocaust denial group), the Conservative Citizens Council, the New Century Foundation, and the National Organization for European American Rights. Such groups can more easily attract Americans who do not think of themselves as racist, but are nevertheless upset over racial preferences, black-on-white crime, and immigration policies that are seen as detrimental to Euro-American interests. Casual listeners are unlikely to be alarmed or tipped off about a friend or colleague's affiliation with such groups since their names raise no red flags.

Racism in the movement

White nationalist organizations espousing racial hatred or racial separatism can hide among such groups, many of which have been newly legitimized by America's embrace of identity politics and widespread acceptance of ethnic group pride. Groups with names like European/American Issues Forum or the National Organization for European American Rights can more easily find mainstream acceptance in a milieu in which we now have Asian American, Hispanic American, and Welsh American advocacy groups. White identity groups, critics would charge, are the next logical expansion of a multiculturalism run amok.

U.S. [white nationalist] groups have found a ready demand for their literature overseas.

In an effort to expand their base, certain white nationalists have also broadened their list of issues and concerns to include an array of topics of interest to many mainstream social and religious conservatives. Loretta J. Ross, director for the Center for Democratic Renewal, reports that some white nationalists have combined traditional racist, white supremacist, and anti-Semitic beliefs with opposition to homosexuality, condemnation of abortion, support for family values, and a strong pro-American foreign policy. "This broadening of issues and the use of conservative buzzwords," Ross writes, "has attracted the attention of whites who may not consider themselves racists, but do consider themselves patriotic Americans concerned about the moral decay of their country."

Potential converts to white nationalism can be found among the millions of frustrated white Americans who have supported mainstream conservative political candidates and the conservative racial policies of presidents Richard Nixon,

Ronald Reagan, and the elder George Bush. Republicans have repeatedly demonstrated the party's ability to attract a significant majority of white votes whenever it champions racially tinged issues such as welfare and immigration reform, affirmative action, and crime reduction. Many of these Republican supporters have been attracted to the party's racially conservative campaigns and policies out of a concern and belief that the interests of white people are being trampled on by an insensitive government, a theme common among white nationalists.

The ability of white nationalists to pass themselves off as mainstream conservatives is well illustrated by the case of Samuel Francis. Francis, a former journalist for the influential conservative newspaper the *Washington Times*, moved freely in conservative circles until his white nationalist views were first exposed in 1995 in D'Souza's *The End of Racism*. "What we as whites must do," Francis proclaimed at Jared Taylor's first *American Renaissance* conference, "is reassert our identity and our solidarity, and we must do so in explicitly racial terms through the articulation of a racial consciousness as whites." "The civilization that we as whites created in Europe and America could not have developed apart from the genetic endowments of the creating people, nor is there any reason to believe that the civilization can be successfully transmitted to a different people."

Francis's exposure as a racial nationalist eventually led to the loss of his job at the *Times*. Bitter over this, he would later complain that a small number of liberal zealots in America could silence the many white people who sympathized with the white nationalist viewpoint. He seemed to be equally angry with the many white sympathizers who shared his own beliefs and goals regarding race, but remained silent and immobilized for fear of retaliation. . . .

Another factor in the expanding influence of the white nationalist message is the ability of many of the newer groups on the racist right to forge alliances with like-minded whites in Europe, Canada, and elsewhere. As Kaplan and Weinberg explain, common conditions have brought together forces on both sides of the Atlantic, resulting in a united desire to maintain a common racial identity that transcends national boundaries. These conditions include demographic pressures, social dislocations, and economic changes. In addition, U.S. groups have found a ready demand for their racist literature overseas, since such literature often cannot be legally published in Europe, where more restricted views of free speech prevail than in America.

9

White Nationalism Is a Solution, Not a Problem

Don Black, interviewed by Russell K. Nieli

Don Black, a former Grand Dragon of the Ku Klux Klan, is now the publisher of the Stormfront Web site, which serves as the nucleus of the white nationalist movement.

Don Black's Stormfront Web site is the mouthpiece for a white nationalist movement that believes all multi-racial societies are destined to fail. The movement advocates a separate white nation and foresees a future America where each race would be sectioned off in a particular area. Black recognizes, though, that a separate white nation is a long-term goal. Of more immediate concern are issues like the Jewish control of the media, interracial marriage, and immigration policies that are draining the wealth and pride of the country. At the heart of the white nationalist movement is the belief that there are inherent differences among the races and that whites have a right to preserve their heritage.

INTERVIEWER: In March 1995, you launched the *Stormfront* website. Could you explain what *Stormfront* is and what you hope to accomplish by it?

BLACK: *Stormfront* is a resource for a movement which we call white nationalism. Our purpose is to provide an alternative news media with news and information and online forums for those who are part of our movement or for those who are interested in learning more about white nationalism. And we believe that the basis for our movement is the fact that white people throughout the world have the right to organize and to

Don Black, interviewed by Russell K. Nieli, "Don Black," *Contemporary Voices of White Nationalism in America*, edited by Carol M. Swain. Cambridge, UK: Cambridge University Press, 2003. Copyright © 2003 by Carol M. Swain and Russ Nieli. Reproduced by permission of the publisher.

promote their heritage and their cultural values, just as every other race and ethnic group has been doing for years. *Storm-front* began in 1991 as an online bulletin board, a dial-in bulletin board, during one of the David Duke campaigns—the David Duke for U.S. Senate campaign. The purpose of the bulletin board system, or BBS, was simply to provide those participants in that campaign who had their own computers and modems and knew how to use them with the ability to exchange messages and files. At that time, we had very few users because there were very few people who had the equipment or were savvy enough to understand how to use it.

It was with the exponential growth of the Internet, which began, I think, in '94 or '95, that we first had the opportunity to reach potentially millions of people with our point of view. These are people who for the most part have never attended one of our meetings or have never subscribed to any of our publications. We were for the first time able to reach a broad audience. And *Stormfront*, being the first white nationalist website, was able immediately to draw a very large number of visitors. The response has continued to grow until this day. And in the future, with the advent of broadband technology for consumers, we hope to be able to compete with television networks themselves by providing an alternative video—video both on demand and in real time—with full motion and full resolution. So the Net has certainly provided our movement, and other movements like ours with only limited resources, with the ability for the first time to compete with what we consider to be a very biased and controlled news media.

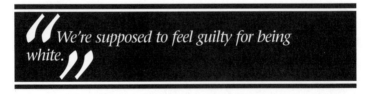

We're supposed to feel guilty for being white.

INTERVIEWER: Who controls the news media and how would you characterize its bias?

BLACK: Well, the bias is certainly directed against the white majority in this country and toward white culture throughout the world, where white people are typically characterized as being oppressors and exploiters of other races. We're supposed to feel guilty for being white. There's an attempt to instill guilt in our people because of our history and our heritage, whereas, on the other side, racial minorities in this country who are non-whites are typically portrayed as being intelligent, sensitive, and often the victims of white oppression. So there is a liberal bias.

And this liberal bias in the media, I think, is caused by several things, not the least of which is the disproportionate Jewish influence. This influence is particularly prominent in television—and particularly television in Hollywood—but it is also present in newspapers, magazines, and other print publications. The Jewish culture has typically taken a very liberal point of view, and throughout most of its history, it has assumed an aloof attitude toward white Western civilization and frequently a very hostile attitude. In the twentieth century, Jews gained control of much of the mass media beginning with the motion picture industry. Motion picture technology was originally invented by Thomas Edison. To escape Edison's control of the new technology, Jews left the Northeast and migrated west to Hollywood. Originally all the major motion picture studios were run by Jews of eastern European origin after they left the Northeast to escape Edison's control. So beginning with Hollywood, and then with the broadcast media later, we've seen a very disproportionate Jewish influence, and I think that has resulted in a very biased attitude toward white Western civilization. It is an attitude which does not reflect America's vision of itself, or at least its original vision of itself.

INTERVIEWER: Why did you choose the name "Stormfront"? To many, the term conjures up images of Nazi stormtroopers. Is that the image you want to convey?

BLACK: Well, it could convey a number of things. It could convey any kind of political front—especially a somewhat militant one. But there's also the weather analogy. We believe that the idea of a storm can evoke images of cleansing. Even though tumultuous, a storm ultimately results in a cleansing. So I wouldn't read too much into the name. It's basically just a neat name that has the projected kind of aura that we would like to surround our movement with.

INTERVIEWER: You have web links to neo-Nazi and anti-Semitic websites. Many people hearing the name "Stormfront" and looking at some of the groups that you associate with would assume that you were a neo-Nazi and rabidly anti-Semitic group. Would that be a correct perception?

BLACK: Well, the term "anti-Semitic," like "Nazi," is one of those words that really is a term of abuse and intended to stifle discussion. We're certainly going to talk about Jewish influence over our media, over our government, and over our foreign policy, and we are certainly going to discuss the real history of World War II. That doesn't mean that we are Nazis, but we are certainly going to be called that among other things as a matter of course by our opposition. As for our links, I'm not sure which specific links you would consider neo-Nazi, but certainly we link to a number of sites that take a differing approach than ours. But we feel that they are all, all the ones we link to, are of value and are of interest to those who might visit *Stormfront*. To answer your question, no, I don't consider myself a Nazi, but that's a term that's frequently applied to us and it's not entirely accurate. It's like calling every liberal a communist. No one gets away with that in the mainstream media today, but they routinely get away with it when referring to us.

> *[White nationalists] believe segregation certainly didn't work, and the only long-term solution to racial conflict is separation.*

INTERVIEWER: Would you also reject the term "white supremacist"?

BLACK: I think that's an inaccurate description of most of the people that are part of our movement because white supremacy implies a system, such as we had throughout most of this country through the fifties and early sixties, in which there was legally enforced segregation and in which whites were in a position of domination. We did have a supremacist-type government in most states, but today the people who are attracted to the white nationalist movement want separation. And so supremacy really isn't descriptive of what we want, the changes we want to see.

INTERVIEWER: What sort of changes then do you want?

BLACK: We are separatists. We believe that we as white people, as European Americans, have the right to pursue our destiny without interference from other races. And we feel that other races have that right as well—the right to develop a nation with a government which reflects their interest and their values without domination or any other interference from whites. We believe segregation certainly didn't work, and the only long-term solution to racial conflict is separation. As long as races are forced together by government, there will continue to be racial hatred and mutual animosity caused by one side or the other feeling that they are being discriminated against. As Thomas Jefferson said, "Nothing is more certainly written in the book of faith than that these people are to be free, nor is it less certain that equally free, they cannot live under the same government. Nature has an opinion. It's drawn indelible lines of distinction between them."

INTERVIEWER: "These people" were the slaves, the black slaves?

BLACK: That's right. That was the context of his writing, and that was in his autobiography. The first half of that statement, the first sentence, is what is inscribed on the Jefferson Memorial to deliberately misrepresent what Jefferson believed. Apparently, the memorial commission shortly after World War II didn't think that anybody would have access to the original autobiography . . . but they didn't bank on the Internet, so now anybody can find it.

INTERVIEWER: Jefferson, you are saying, basically believed what you now believe, namely, that an integrated society in America that includes both blacks and whites is impossible?

BLACK: Right. Almost all of the founding fathers believed that. They even founded an organization called the American Colonization Society whose purpose was to free black slaves and repatriate them to Africa. And, of course, the nation of Liberia, with its capital named after James Monroe, Monrovia, was a result of that, too. But this part of our history is now hidden from most students going through our school systems today because it's not politically fashionable. People like Thomas Jefferson, George Washington, and James Monroe spoke out forcefully on the issue of race, but that part of their philosophy is simply ignored. And, of course, in the case of Jefferson, he is being vilified with the Sally Hemmings accusations, which have not been proven despite what's been said in the press. You know, I firmly believe that the television, the television dramatization and all of the earlier media frenzy over the Sally Hemmings affair is a result of what Thomas Jefferson said about race. What he said about race is unacceptable to many. *Stormfront*, in particular, has done its best to bring to the attention of the American people the truth about Jefferson's beliefs on race. And I really believe that this vilification of Thomas Jefferson is a direct result of that awareness. I may be a little bit paranoid on this. But I really believe that that's a big part of it.

INTERVIEWER: You describe yourself as a racial separatist.

Could you explain your vision for the future of America in terms of race?

BLACK: I think part of America . . . part of this continent will be a white nation. That's what we want to see ultimately. In the short run, we want to see the government get out of the business of race mixing, get out of the business of forcing races together, and of telling employers who they can hire, who they must hire, and who they must promote, telling schools how they have to run their business, and telling people where they have to live or who they have to live with. And I think left to their own devices, members of most races will separate naturally. I think most people of whatever race prefer to live and work and go to school with people who share their background and their values.

We want a separate white nation.

INTERVIEWER: So you oppose antidiscrimination laws?

BLACK: Yes, I do. Not only do we oppose antidiscrimination laws, we also oppose affirmative action, which are prodiscrimination laws, in which white people are the people who are discriminated against. But we don't think that government has any business telling businesses who they have to hire. We don't think that they have any business telling neighborhoods, or real estate people, who they have to sell to, and we believe that if people want to go to a school that's all white or all black, they have that right as well.

INTERVIEWER: What sort of racial separation would you want to see in the distant future? Would you want to see America broken up into different ethnic enclaves?

BLACK: Well, you know, I think that's going to happen. Yes, I want to see separation. That's the whole fundamental premise of white nationalism. We want a separate white nation. But regardless of what I want, I think it's going to happen. In some areas, specifically in the Southwest, there are many nonwhite Hispanics, mestizos, and Indian Hispanics who are loyal to Mexico rather than the United States and who want to take the southwestern United States back and rejoin Mexico. This is a serious movement, and I think it will continue to grow and gain influence, and at some point in the next twenty years, I believe that we will actually see a physical seizure of that part of the United States. And I don't think that the government in Washington, which is becoming an imperial government, is going to be able to do much about it. So at that point, there will likely be other races who will decide they want to do the same thing, and at some point, European Americans will have to realize that they must defend their own interests as well.

INTERVIEWER: If the Southwest became an Hispanic state, where geographically would the European American state be located?

BLACK: Well, that remains to be seen. I don't know just how this is going to work out, but the broadest expanse of predominantly white populated area in this country, of course, is in the Northwest. But I don't know that that is where we will end up.

INTERVIEWER: Where would Asians fit into this picture? And Arabs?

BLACK: Well, our purpose is to see the development of an all-white nation. I don't know where Asians are going to go or where Arabs are going to go, but our purpose is simply to provide white people with their own territory with defensible borders. The history of the world is one of migration and conquest, and I'm sure that is going to continue. But I don't have a plan for everybody in the world. We only have a plan for ourselves, the white people, and at some point we believe that it will become obvious to most of our fellow whites that an all-white nation is necessary somewhere on this continent.

INTERVIEWER: Most Jews in the United States are Ashkenazic Jews from Europe. Would they be part of that white nation?

BLACK: No.

INTERVIEWER: Why not?

BLACK: Well, most Jews aren't going to want to be a part of that white nation, for one thing. Probably 90 percent of Jews have a very liberal attitude toward race and have been very much a part of the multicultural movement to turn everybody into one homogenized brown mass. But the Jews are a distinct racial and cultural group—many Jews themselves stress their separateness.

INTERVIEWER: How does that differ from Italian Americans who have a high level of ethnic identity?

BLACK: The Italians and Irishmen and other European nationalities have shared the same general culture, and they are assimilable from the cultural and racial standpoint, whereas Jews are not. Jews have not assimilated over the last few thousand years despite living among a variety of nations.

INTERVIEWER: What about the high level of intermarriage? The intermarriage rates—the out-marriage rate—among Jews is estimated to be about 50 percent. Wouldn't that suggest a willingness to assimilate?

BLACK: Well, if that's true, why do we have the state of Israel? The only real, truly nationalist state—a religious and race-based national state—is Israel, and obviously the Jewish leadership, which supports Israel, doesn't feel that assimilation is very desirable. And that 50 percent assimilation rate, I question the accuracy of that because I don't think Jews are in any danger of disappearing from the planet, as they well would be if the rate truly were 50 percent, given the fact that Jews have about the same birthrate as whites, which is below the level needed to maintain the existing population. Jewish nationalism is a major force, and while the assimilation movement is probably going to have some effect on Jewish numbers, it's by no means going to result in the assimilation of the race.

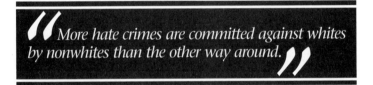

More hate crimes are committed against whites by nonwhites than the other way around.

INTERVIEWER: Is your aversion primarily to Jewish liberalism or to all Jews? Many Jews certainly are not liberal—important segments of the Jewish population are anything but liberal.

BLACK: But most Jews are liberal, and there is a racial and religious cohesiveness which extends beyond their particular politics. I've certainly known many Jews who agree with most of what we have to say, but they are a very small minority, and they are not part of the Jewish mainstream. They are not the people who control the TV networks and the banking system, and they are really not calling the shots.

INTERVIEWER: You were quoted in an article in the February 1998 issue of *New Times* magazine as saying, and here I quote: "A multicultural Yugoslav nation can't hold up for too long. Whites won't have any choice but to take military action. It's our children whose interests we have to defend." This sounds like a violent, bloody picture. Do you envision violence on the horizon here and military actions?

BLACK: I think that is certainly possible. There's a lot of violence right now. There is a lot of racial crime now, and, contrary to the media's portrayal of hate crimes, more hate crimes are committed against whites by nonwhites than the other way around. And I think we are going to see that kind of thing continue. I think there will be more racial strife, and I would much prefer that it not reach the point of what's happened in the Balkans, but that could happen. That's a possibility if the current policy of our government to set itself up as some sort of imperial government in which it controls these diverse racial and cultural groups continues. . . .

INTERVIEWER: You have expressed strong disapproval of both antidiscrimination policies on the part of the state, as well as affirmative action policies—policies of racial and ethnic preferences. Are these the government policies that you find most galling and most destructive, or are there other government policies which you find harmful . . . harmful to race relations, anyway?

BLACK: The government policy we find most detrimental in the long term, of course, is the government's immigration policy, in which Third World immigrants are allowed to come to this country, either legally or illegally. Of course, these millions of people who come here every year have resulted in many parts of the United States coming to resemble a Third World country. Of course, this is the kind of thing that's much more difficult to reverse than just a set of laws, such as affirmative action and other laws of that type. So immigration would be the single most destructive policy that's implemented by the government.

Of course, there are other issues that concern us—the domination of our foreign policy by un-American interests is of concern to us. The recent bombing of Serbia, which was a sovereign nation which had done nothing to the United States, was unprecedented and morally outrageous and will likely result in many people throughout the world hating the United States even more than in the past. The subjugation of our foreign policy to the state of Israel is another example of an issue that would be of concern to us. Half of our foreign aid budget goes to either Israel or to Egypt to keep peace with Israel. Our military and all of our policies in the Middle East are oriented toward protecting Israel, and that's something else that's probably unprecedented in the history of the world—where such a small nation has managed to dominate the foreign policy of a world superpower.

Obviously there are many issues that concern us. The tax

system we have and the welfare system we have in this country concerns us. A tax system designed to support a welfare system which encourages the welfare underclass to continue to grow is obviously wrong. But these are all policies that can be changed very quickly. The immigration policy is something whose consequences are much more long lasting.

INTERVIEWER: What sort of immigration reform would you like to see passed?

BLACK: Well, in the 1920s the United States passed its first broad immigration laws, which favored Europeans based on the fact that most Americans considered this to be a country whose heritage was European. Ensuring that immigration was limited to Europeans was a very logical thing. And, of course, we believe the same thing as the immigration reformers of the 1920s. This is not a melting pot, except for European nationalities, who are able to melt because they share a general culture. This isn't a country in which every race from every continent with every culture can just assimilate without serious problems. We believe that we have the right to maintain a nation which reflects its original European values and culture.

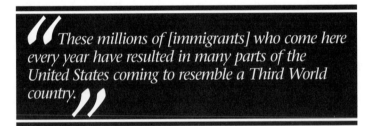

These millions of [immigrants] who come here every year have resulted in many parts of the United States coming to resemble a Third World country.

INTERVIEWER: Surely there are great differences between many of the European ethnic groups in terms of their own national cultures. The Irish peasant culture, the French urban culture, the Polish rural cultures—these are very different cultures, and yet people have been able to form some kind of common core American values coming from these disparate backgrounds. Why can't this process of assimilation be expanded to include African Americans and Japanese and Jews and Chinese and so on?

BLACK: Because the gulf with those groups is simply too great, particularly with Africans and with the mestizo and Amerindian Hispanic cultures, and with Asians as well, but to a lesser degree. But certainly there are some profound differences between European nationalities and between economic classes within those nationalities, but those differences are dwarfed when compared with the differences between races. The question is why is this so desirable anyway? It's really not diversity, it's antidiversity when one promotes the mixing and homogenation of every race. From that standpoint, we at *Stormfront* are the true promoters of diversity because we want to see our race preserved, as well as every other race, as a distinct cultural entity. Why is there such an imperative to bring everybody together into one society where they are all going to somehow assimilate, where they are going to be equal and the same. It simply doesn't work, but even if it did, what's the point? Why do we have to do this?

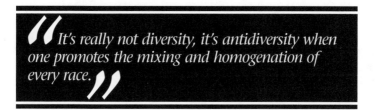

It's really not diversity, it's antidiversity when one promotes the mixing and homogenation of every race.

INTERVIEWER: What are your views on interracial marriage? I mentioned already the Jews. With the Japanese, the story is similar. About half of Japanese men, it has been estimated, marry non-Asian women, usually Caucasians.

BLACK: Well, we're obviously opposed to interracial marriage since it further threatens the integrity of our race and culture. Many members of other races are probably even more opposed to it than we are. I'm not familiar with the figures regarding Japanese men, but I know that many members of, many members of other races also would like to maintain the integrity of their race as well, and see interracial marriage as being very harmful. Yeah, there's a lot of intermixture between Asians and whites because aesthetically they see themselves as somewhat similar, and mentally they are pretty close, whereas these same people would never consider marrying a black person because they see the blacks as being different than them. They see their mental abilities as being less than theirs. But Caucasians and Asians—northern Asians, at least—evolved somewhat along the same lines, and they developed somewhat similar social mores, culture, and mental abilities.

INTERVIEWER: So northern Asians and whites, you are suggesting, have a great deal more in common than whites do with blacks, and for that reason you think they intermarry more often?

BLACK: Right. I don't agree with intermarriage, but that's clearly the reason that it's much more common between Asians and whites than between blacks and whites or Hispanics and whites.

INTERVIEWER: *Stormfront* is routinely characterized by its critics, including the Southern Poverty Law Center, the Anti-Defamation League of the B'nai B'rith, and HateWatch, as racist. What do you say to such characterizations?

BLACK: Well, "racist" is another one of these scare words that doesn't have any real meaning. I certainly believe in race. I am a racialist, but I reject the term "racist" because it is a word that was invented by our opposition. In fact, it was first used by Leon Trotsky in a speech in the early twenties, but really didn't become popular until the fifties and sixties. So I reject the term "racist" simply because of the connotations that have been ascribed to it by our opposition. But I believe in racial differences, and from that standpoint maybe you could call me a racist, but that's not a term that I accept.

INTERVIEWER: What term do you prefer to use to describe your philosophy?

BLACK: Well, the traditional word was "racialist" for anyone who believed in racial differences. That's the traditional construction. I know this sounds a little pedantic to some people; in fact, I just responded to a threat on our message board about this very subject—racialist vs. racist—but the thing is, words are important, and the impression they carry is very important. I think "racist" became popular among our opposition instead of the word "racialist" simply because it's got this hiss to it. It actually sounds evil, and I really believe that these kinds of things in a propaganda war are very important. And, of course, we are losing the propaganda war, and that's one of the reasons—because we have these words ascribed to us which carry connotations which are not true but nevertheless sound very offensive to the kinds of people whom we would like to attract to our cause. So racialist is a legitimate word, and it's a traditional word for those who believe in racial differences. We go a little beyond that because we are also white nationalists in that we want a separate white nation.

10

Racism Is a Significant Global Problem

Martin Jacques

Martin Jacques, former editor of the British magazine Marxism Today, *is a visiting fellow at the London School of Economics. The death of his Indian Malaysian wife, Harinder Veriah, in 2000, in a Hong Kong hospital was blamed on racist lack of medical attention from the Chinese staff toward the dark-skinned patient. The incident triggered an outcry that culminated in an announcement by the Hong Kong government that it would introduce antiracist legislation for the first time.*

It can be very difficult for whites to understand racism because they have never experienced it personally. Over the last five hundred years, colonization and slavery have reinforced the global hierarchy of race that still exists today. This is the reason whites are afforded privileged status while traveling internationally, while nonwhites are often subjected to overt racism. By and large, white leaders have been unable—or unwilling—to recognize this on the international stage. Unless that changes, the hope of securing equality for all races is remote.

I always found race difficult to understand. It was never intuitive. And the reason was simple. Like every other white person, I had never experienced it myself: the meaning of colour was something I had to learn. The turning point was falling in love with my wife, an Indian-Malaysian, and her coming to live in England. Then, over time, I came to see my own country in a completely different way, through her eyes, her background. Colour is something white people never have to think about because for them it is never a handicap, never a source of prejudice or discrimination, but rather the opposite, a source of privilege. However liberal and enlightened I tried to be, I still had a white outlook on the world. My wife was the beginning of my education.

> *Every race displays racial prejudice, is capable of racism, carries assumptions about its own virtue and superiority.*

But it was not until we went to live in Hong Kong that my view of the world, and the place that race occupies within it, was to be utterly transformed. Rather than seeing race through the prism of my own society, I learned to see it globally. When we left these shores, it felt as if we were moving closer to my wife's world: this was east Asia and she was Malaysian. And she, unlike me, had the benefit of speaking Cantonese. So my expectation was that she would feel more comfortable in this environment than I would. I was wrong. As a white, I found myself treated with respect and deference, my wife, notwithstanding her knowledge of the language and her intimacy with Chinese culture, was the object of an in-your-face racism.

Global racial hierarchy

In our 14 months in Hong Kong, I learned some brutal lessons about racism. First, it is not the preserve of whites. Every race displays racial prejudice, is capable of racism, carries assumptions about its own virtue and superiority. Each racism, furthermore, is subtly different, reflecting the specificity of its own culture and history.

Second, there is a global racial hierarchy that helps to shape the power and the prejudices of each race. At the top of this hierarchy are whites. The reasons are deep-rooted and profound. White societies have been the global top dogs for half a millennium, ever since Chinese civilisation went into decline. With global hegemony, first with Europe and then the US, whites have long commanded respect, as well as arousing fear and resentment, among other races. Being white confers a privilege, a special kind of deference, throughout the world, be it

Kingston, Hong Kong, Delhi, Lagos. . . . Whites are the only race that never suffers any kind of systemic racism anywhere in the world. And the impact of white racism has been far more profound and baneful than any other: it remains the only racism with global reach.

Being top of the pile means that whites are peculiarly and uniquely insensitive to race and racism, and the power relations this involves. We are invariably the beneficiaries, never the victims. Even when well-meaning, we remain strangely ignorant. The clout enjoyed by whites does not reside simply in an abstraction—western societies—but in the skin of each and every one of us. Whether we like it or not, in every corner of the planet we enjoy an extraordinary personal power bestowed by our colour. It is something we are largely oblivious of, and consequently take for granted, irrespective of whether we are liberal or reactionary, backpackers, tourists or expatriate businessmen.

The existence of a de facto global racial hierarchy helps to shape the nature of racial prejudice exhibited by other races. Whites are universally respected, even when that respect is combined with strong resentment. A race generally defers to those above it in the hierarchy and is contemptuous of those below it. The Chinese—like the Japanese—widely consider themselves to be number two in the pecking order and look down upon all other races as inferior. Their respect for whites is also grudging— many Chinese believe that western hegemony is, in effect, held on no more than prolonged leasehold. Those below the Chinese and the Japanese in the hierarchy are invariably people of colour (both Chinese and Japanese often like to see themselves as white, or nearly white). At the bottom of the pile, virtually everywhere it would seem, are those of African descent, the only exception in certain cases being the indigenous peoples.

The importance of skin colour

This highlights the centrality of colour to the global hierarchy. Other factors serve to define and reinforce a race's position in the hierarchy—levels of development, civilisational values, history, religion, physical characteristics and dress—but the most insistent and widespread is colour. The reason is that colour is instantly recognisable, it defines difference at the glance of an eye. It also happens to have another effect. It makes the global hierarchy seem like the natural order of things: you are born with your colour, it is something nobody can do anything about, it is neither cultural nor social but physical in origin. In the era of globalisation, with mass migration and globalised cultural industries, colour has become the universal calling card of difference. In interwar Europe, the dominant forms of racism were anti-semitism and racialised nationalisms, today it is colour: at a football match, it is blacks not Jews that get jeered, even in eastern Europe.

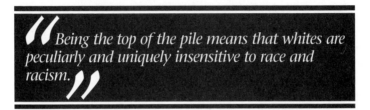

Being the top of the pile means that whites are peculiarly and uniquely insensitive to race and racism.

Liberals like to think that racism is a product of ignorance, of a lack of contact, and that as human mobility increases, so racism will decline. This might be described as the Benetton view of the world. And it does contain a modicum of truth. Intermixing can foster greater understanding, but not necessarily, as Burnley [England], Sri Lanka and Israel, in their very different ways, all testify. Hong Kong, compared with China, is an open society, and has long been so, yet it has had little or no effect in mollifying Chinese prejudice towards people of darker skin. It is not that racism is immovable and intractable, but that its roots are deep, its prejudices as old as humanity itself. The origins of Chinese racism lie in the Middle Kingdom: the belief that the Chinese are superior to other races—with the exception of whites—is centuries, if not thousands of years, old. The disparaging attitude among American whites towards blacks has its roots in slavery. Wishing it wasn't true, denying it is true, will never change the reality. We can only understand—and tackle racism—if we are honest about it. And when it comes to race—more than any other issue—honesty is in desperately short supply.

Unspoken racism

Race remains the great taboo. Take the case of Hong Kong. A conspiracy of silence surrounded race. As the British deported in 1997, amid much self-congratulation, they breathed not a word about racism. Yet the latter was integral to colonial rule, its leitmotif: colonialism, after all, is institutionalised racism at its crudest and most base. The majority of Chinese, the object of it, meanwhile, harboured an equally racist mentality towards people of darker skin. Masters of their own home, they too are in denial of their own racism. But that, in varying degrees, is true of racism not only in Hong Kong but in every country in the world. You may remember that, after the riots in Burnley, in the summer of 2001, [Prime Minister] Tony Blair declared that they were not a true reflection of the state of race relations in Britain: of course, they were, even if the picture is less discouraging in other aspects.

Racism everywhere remains largely invisible and hugely under-estimated, the issue that barely speaks its name. How can the *Economist* produce a 15,000-word survey on migration, as it did in 2002, and hardly mention the word racism? Why does virtually no one talk about the racism suffered by the Williams sisters on the tennis circuit even though the evidence is legion? Why are the deeply racist western attitudes towards Arabs barely mentioned in the context of the occupation of Iraq, carefully hidden behind talk of religion and civilisational values?

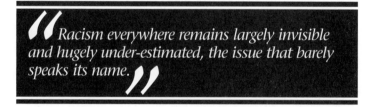

Racism everywhere remains largely invisible and hugely under-estimated, the issue that barely speaks its name.

The dominant race in a society, whether white or otherwise, rarely admits to its own racism. Denial is near universal. The reasons are manifold. It has a huge vested interest in its own privilege. It will often be oblivious to its own prejudices. It will regard its racist attitudes as nothing more than common sense, having the force and justification of nature. Only when challenged by those on the receiving end is racism outed, and attitudes begin to change. The reason why British society is less nakedly racist than it used to be is that whites have been forced by people of colour to question age-old racist assumptions. Nations are never honest about themselves: they are all in varying degrees of denial.

This is clearly fundamental to understanding the way in which racism is underplayed as a national and global issue. But there is another reason, which is a specifically white problem. Because whites remain the overwhelmingly dominant global race, perched in splendid isolation on top of the pile even though they only represent 17% of the world's population, they are overwhelmingly responsible for setting the global agenda, for determining what is discussed and what is not. And the fact that whites have no experience of racism, except as perpetrators, means that racism is constantly underplayed by western institutions—by governments, by the media, by corporations. Moreover, because whites have reigned globally supreme for half a millennium, they, more than any other race, have left their mark on the rest of humanity: they have a vested interest in denying the extent and baneful effects of racism.

It was only [in 2001] . . . that the first-ever United Nations conference on racism was held—against the fierce resistance of the US (and that in the [President] Clinton era). Nothing more eloquently testifies to the unwillingness of western governments to engage in a global dialogue about the problem of racism.

If racism is now more widely recognised than it used to be, the situation is likely to be transformed over the next few decades. As migration increases, as the regime of denial is challenged, as subordinate races find the will and confidence to challenge the dominant race, as understanding of racism develops, as we become more aware of other racisms like that of the Han Chinese, then the global prominence of racism is surely set to increase dramatically.

It is rare to hear a political leader speaking the discourse of colour. Robert Mugabe [president of Zimbabwe] is one, but he is tainted and discredited. The Malaysian prime minister, Mahathir Mohamed, is articulate on the subject of white privilege and the global hierarchy. The most striking example by a huge margin, though, is [South Africa's] Nelson Mandela. When it comes to colour, his sacrifice is beyond compare and his authority unimpeachable. And his message is always universal—not confined to the interests of one race. It is he who has suggested that western support for Israel has something to do with race. It is he who has hinted that it is no accident that the authority of the UN is under threat at a time when its secretary general is black. And yet his voice is almost alone in a world where race oozes from every pore of humanity. In a world where racism is becoming increasingly important, we will need more such leaders. And invariably they will be people of colour: on this subject whites lack moral authority. I could only understand the racism suffered by my wife through her words and experience. I never felt it myself. The difference is utterly fundamental.

Organizations to Contact

The editors have compiled the following list of organizations concerned with the issues debated in this book. The descriptions are derived from materials provided by the organizations. All have publications or information available for interested readers. The list was compiled on the date of publication of the present volume; names, addresses, phone and fax numbers, and e-mail addresses may change. Be aware that many organizations take several weeks or longer to respond to inquiries, so allow as much time as possible.

American Civil Liberties Union (ACLU)
125 Broad St., 18th Fl. New York, NY 10004
(212) 944-9800
Web site: www.aclu.org

The ACLU is a nonprofit, nonpartisan membership organization founded in 1920 to support and vigorously defend individual civil liberties as guaranteed in the Constitution, particularly the rights of free speech and assembly, equal protection, privacy, and separation of church and state. It handles constitutional challenges and works to extend civil rights to minorities and the poor, prisoners, women, and the disabled through some six thousand court cases annually. Its Web site offers an archive of landmark Supreme Court decisions in which the ACLU played a role as direct counsel, an online newsletter of ACLU activities, and a range of roundtable discussions and audio chats on protecting civil liberties even in times of national emergency.

Anti-Defamation League (ADL)
823 United Nations Plaza, New York, NY 10017
(212) 490-2525
Web site: www.adl.org

The charter of the ADL, founded in 1913, states, "The immediate object of the league is to stop, by appeals to reason and conscience and, if necessary, by appeals to law, the defamation of the Jewish people. Its ultimate purpose is to secure justice and fair treatment to all citizens alike." The ADL monitors global anti-Semitism, sponsors national and international interfaith conferences, lobbies elected officials in support of the State of Israel, and publishes an online catalog of classroom and community resources.

Center for Equal Opportunity
14 Pidgeon Hill Dr., Suite 500, Sterling, VA 20165
(703) 421-5443
e-mail: comment@ceousa.org • Web site: www.ceousa.org

A nonpartisan think tank devoted exclusively to the promotion of color-blind equal opportunity and racial harmony, the Center for Equal

Opportunity aims to counter the divisive impact of race-conscious public policies. The center focuses on three areas in particular: racial preferences, immigration and assimilation, and multicultural education.

Center for the Study of White American Culture
245 W. Fourth Ave., Roselle, NJ 07203
(908) 241-5439
e-mail: contact@euroamerican.org • Web site: www.euroamerican.org

In 1995 a white American man and an African American woman founded the Center for the Study of White American Culture to examine white American culture in the context of the greater American culture. Explicitly a multiracial organization, the center's founding principle is that a complete examination of white American culture must include the perspectives of both insiders and outsiders of that culture.

Columbia Workshop on Journalism, Race & Ethnicity
Columbia Graduate School of Journalism
2950 Broadway, New York, NY 10027
(212) 854-5377
e-mail: am494@columbia.edu
Web site: www.jrn.columbia.edu

The aim of the Columbia University workshop is to encourage candid and complete coverage of race and ethnicity, illuminate racial and ethnic controversy, puncture stereotypes, and stir community dialogue through responsible journalism. The workshop publishes a best-practices guidebook for editors, journalists, and educators; its Web site is a good resource for links addressing racial bias in the print and broadcast media.

Environmental Justice Resource Center (EJRC) at Clark Atlanta University
223 James P. Brawley Dr., Atlanta, GA 30314
(404) 880-6911
e-mail: ejrc@cau.edu • Web site: www.ejrc.cau.edu

The center was formed in 1994 to serve as a research, policy, and information clearinghouse on issues related to environmental justice, race and the environment, civil rights, facility siting, land use planning, brownfields, transportation equity, suburban sprawl, and smart growth. The overall goal of the center is to assist, support, train, and educate people of color, students, professionals, and grassroots community leaders to participate in the mainstream of environmental decision making.

International Movement Against All Forms of Discrimination and Racism (IMADR)
Geneva, Switzerland
(41) 22-791-6263
e-mail: imadris@imadr.org • Web site: www.imadr.org

IMADR is an international nonprofit, nongovernmental human rights organization devoted to eliminating all forms of discrimination around the world, forging international solidarity among discriminated minorities and advancing the international regime of human rights. Founded in 1988 by one of Japan's largest minorities, the Burakumin, IMADR has grown to be a global network of concerned citizens and minority groups with regional committees in Asia, North America, Latin America, and Europe. IMADR is in consultative status with the United Nations Economic and Social Council (ECOSOC).

National Association for the Advancement of Colored People (NAACP)
4805 Mt. Hope Dr., Baltimore, MD 21215
(410) 521-4939
e-mail: washingtonbureau@naacpnet.org • Web site: www.naacp.org

The NAACP works to ensure the political, educational, social, and economic equality of minority groups and citizens; achieve equal rights and eliminate race prejudice among the citizens of the United States; remove all barriers of racial discrimination through the democratic processes; enact and enforce federal, state, and local laws securing civil rights; inform the public of the adverse effects of racial discrimination and seek its elimination; educate persons as to their constitutional rights; and take all lawful action to further these aims.

National Council of La Raza (NCLR)
1111 Nineteenth St. NW, Suite 1000, Washington, DC 20036
(202) 785-1670
Web site: www.nclr.org

Established in 1968, NCLR works to reduce poverty and discrimination and improve opportunities for Hispanic Americans. The council's activities focus on applied research, policy analysis, advocacy, and supporting and strengthening Hispanic community-based organizations.

National Rainbow/PUSH Coalition
930 E. Fiftieth St., Chicago, IL 60615-2702
(773) 373-3366
e-mail: info@rainbowpush.org • Web site: www.rainbowpush.org

The National Rainbow/PUSH Coalition is a multiracial, multi-issue, international membership organization founded by Rev. Jesse L. Jackson Sr. From its national headquarters in Chicago and a bureau in Washington, D.C., the coalition seeks to attract people of diverse ethnic, religious, economic, and political backgrounds to eliminate racism and support a liberal, social, and political agenda.

National Urban League
120 Wall St., 8th Fl., New York, NY 10005
(212) 558-5300
e-mail: info@nul.org • Web site: www.nul.org

The Urban League is the nation's oldest and largest community-based movement devoted to empowering African Americans to enter the economic and social mainstream. Its three-pronged strategy includes ensuring that African American children are well educated, helping adults attain economic self-sufficiency, and promoting civil rights in the community at large.

White Aryan Resistance (WAR)
PO Box 65, Fallbrook, CA 92088
(760) 723-8996
e-mail: warmetzger@aol.com • Web site: www.resist.com

WAR is a white supremacist organization that promotes a fierce brand of anti-Semitic, racist, and anti-immigrant ideology. Leader Tom Metzger cultivates a following through a monthly newspaper, a Web site, a telephone hotline, an e-mail newsletter, and other media.

Bibliography

Books

Molefi K. Asante	*Erasing Racism.* Amherst, NY: Prometheus, 2003.
Edwin Black	*War Against the Weak: Eugenics and America's Campaign to Create a Master Race.* New York: Four Walls Eight Windows, 2003.
Kathleen M. Blee	*Inside Organized Racism: Women in the Hate Movement.* Berkeley and Los Angeles: University of California Press, 2002.
Patrick Buchanan	*The Death of the West: How Dying Populations and Immigrant Invasions Imperil Our Country and Civilization.* New York: Dunne, 2001.
Sheryll Cashin	*The Failure of Integration: How Race and Class Are Undermining the American Dream.* New York: PublicAffairs, 2004.
Arlene M. Davila and Agustin Lao-Montes	*Mambo Montage.* New York: Columbia University Press, 2001.
Betty A. Dobratz and Stephanie L. Shanks-Meile	*The White Separatist Movement in the United States: "White Power, White Pride!"* Baltimore: Johns Hopkins University Press, 2001.
Gerhard Falk	*Stigma: How We Treat Outsiders.* Amherst, NY: Prometheus, 2001.
Joe R. Feagin	*Racist America: Roots, Current Realities, and Future Reparations.* New York: Routledge, 2000.
Henry Louis Gates	*America Behind the Color Line: Dialogues with African Americans.* New York: Warner, 2004.
Andrew Hacker	*Two Nations: Black and White, Separate, Hostile, Unequal.* New York: Scribner, 2003.
Peter Irons	*Jim Crow's Children: The Broken Promise of the Brown Decision.* New York: Viking, 2002.
Randall Kennedy	*Nigger: The Strange Career of a Troublesome Word.* New York: Pantheon, 2002.
Anoop Nayak	*Race, Place and Globalization: Youth Cultures in a Changing World.* New York: Berg, 2003.
Charles J. Ogletree	*All Deliberate Speed: Reflections on the First Half Century of* Brown v. Board of Education. *New York: W.W. Norton, 2004.*

Marco Portales	*Crowding Out Latinos: Mexican Americans in the Public Consciousness.* Philadelphia: Temple University Press, 2000.
Craig R. Prentiss, ed.	*Religion and the Creation of Race and Ethnicity.* New York: New York University Press, 2003.
Nikhil Pal Singh	*Black Is a Country: Race and the Unfinished Struggle for Democracy.* Cambridge, MA: Harvard University Press, 2004.
Hayer Stier and Marta Tienda	*The Color of Opportunity: Pathways to Family, Welfare, and Work.* Chicago: University of Chicago Press, 2001.
Carol M. Swain	*The New White Nationalism in America: Its Challenge to Integration.* Cambridge, UK: Cambridge University Press, 2002.
Carol M. Swain, ed.	*Contemporary Voices of White Nationalism in America.* Cambridge, UK: Cambridge University Press, 2003.
Stephan Talty	*Mulatto America.* New York: HarperCollins, 2003.
Greg Tate	*Everything but the Burden: What White People Are Taking from Black Culture.* New York: Broadway, 2003.
Abigal Thernstrom and Stephan Thernstrom	*America in Black and White: One Nation, Indivisible.* New York: Touchstone, 1999.
Cooper Thompson, Emmett Schaefer, and Harry Brod	*White Men Challenging Racism: 35 Personal Stories.* Durham, NC: Duke University Press, 2003.
Debra Van Ausdale and Joe R. Feagin	*The First R: How Children Learn Race and Racism.* Lanham, MD: Rowman & Littlefield, 2002.
Lena Williams	*It's the Little Things: Everyday Interactions That Anger, Annoy, and Divide the Races.* New York: Harvest, 2002.
Frank H. Wu	*Yellow: Race in America Beyond Black and White.* New York: Basic Books, 2002.

Periodicals

Stanley Aronowitz	"Race: The Continental Divide," *Nation*, March 12, 2001.
Sharon Begley	"The Roots of Hatred," *AARP*, May/June 2004.
John Bragg	"The New Segregation: Racism in America, Then and Now," *Capitalist*, December 19, 2002.
David Brooks	"People Like Us," *Atlantic Monthly*, September 2003.
Fox Butterfield	"Often, Parole Is One Stop on the Way Back to Prison." *New York Times*, November 29, 2000.

Gene Callahan and William Anderson	"The Roots of Racial Profiling: Why Are Police Targeting Minorities for Traffic Stops?" *Reason*, August/September 2001.
Jan M. Chaiken	"Crunching Numbers: Crime and Incarceration at the End of the Millennium," *National Institute of Justice Journal*, January 2000.
Ellis Cose	"The Prison Paradox," *Newsweek*, November 13, 2000.
Jim F. Couch et al.	"Of Racism and Rubbish: The Geography of Race and Pollution in Mississippi," *Independent Review*, Fall 2003.
David Horowitz	"Black Racism: The Hate Crime That Dare Not Speak Its Name," *FrontPageMagazine.com*, July 16, 2002.
Jeff Jacoby	"The Death of American Racism," *Boston Globe*, July 13, 2003.
Martin Jacques	"The Global Hierarchy of Race," *Guardian–Final Edition*, September 20, 2003.
Coretta Scott King	"40 Years Later . . . Have We Overcome Yet?" *Ebony*, August 2003.
Heather Mac Donald	"The Black Cops You Never Hear About," *City Journal*, Summer 2002.
Chris Rice	"Is That Racism on Your Shoe?" *Sojourners*, November/December 2002.
Ron Stodghill and Amanda Bower	"Welcome to America's Most Diverse City," *Time*, August 25, 2002.
Paul Street	"Color Bind: Prisons and the New American Racism," *Dissent*, September 3, 2002.
Derald Wing Sue	"Dismantling the Myth of a Color-Blind Society," *Black Issues in Higher Education*, November 6, 2003.
U.S. Commission on Civil Rights	"Not in My Backyard: Executive Order 12,898 and Title VI as Tools for Achieving Environmental Justice," September 4, 2003.
Women's Quarterly	"What Nobody Wants to Say About Race: Author and Civil Rights Commissioner Abigail Thernstrom talks to Charlotte Hays," Autumn 2001.

Web Sites

Crosspoint Anti-Racism, www.magenta.nl/crosspoint. A comprehensive site that examines global racism and human rights abuses, with links to over two thousand organizations in 114 countries addressing discrimination against indigenous peoples, minorities, women, refugees, and Jews; sponsored by the Magenta Foundation, a nonprofit, nongovernmental organization based in Amsterdam.

Environmental Justice/Environmental Racism, www.ejnet.org/ej. Useful links to government agencies dealing with environmental justice policy, key legal cases related to environmental discrimination in minority communities, and toxic waste site maps.

Hate Crimes Research Network, www.hatecrime.net. Hate Crimes Research Network, based at the Department of Sociology at Portland State University in Oregon, offers links to academic research into bias-motivated crime. The site pools research data for sociologists, psychologists, criminologists, and students.

Southern Poverty Law Center, www.tolerance.org. This Web project of the Southern Poverty Law Center, which monitors and issues reports on hate groups in the United States, promotes tolerance through education and activism. Designed for teachers, parents, and teens, the site offers recommended reading lists, suggestions for school and community projects, and comprehensive archives of news reports on racist incidents and tolerance programs.

White Nationalist Resource Page, www.stormfront.org. The White Nationalist movement advocates segregation of the races, strict immigration controls, and the abolition of affirmative action programs to counter threats to the white race. Its Web site contains anti-Semitic and neo-Nazi tracts that advance white supremacist ideology as necessary to preserve Western culture.

Index